Private

WASHINGTON

✳

Private WASHINGTON

*

RESIDENCES IN THE NATION'S CAPITAL

JAN CIGLIANO PHOTOGRAPHS BY WALTER SMALLING, JR.

Foreword by Sally Quinn

RIZZOLI
NEW YORK

Front and back jacket: The Octagon. William Thornton, architect, 1797–1801

Frontispiece: Library, David Schwarz house, Kalorama.
Ewing & Allen, architects, 1925.

Pages 16–17: The Federalists: Halcyon House, Georgetown, 1787; restoration, 1978.

Pages 58–59: The Romantics: Rendering of the Oatsie Charles house, Georgetown.
Adams & Haskins, architects, 1854.

Pages 86–87: The Academics: David Schwarz house, Kalorama.
Ewing & Allen, architects, 1925.

Pages 144–45: The Moderns: German Ambassador's residence, Foxhall.
Oswald Mathias Ungers, architect, 1994.

Page 192: Theo Adamstein and Olvia Demetriou house, Foxhall, 1940s.

First published in 1998 by
Rizzoli International Publications, Inc.
300 Park Avenue South, New York, N.Y. 10010

Library of Congress Cataloging-in-Publication Data
Cigliano, Jan
        Private Washington : residences in the nation's capital / Jan
    Cigliano; photographs by Walter Smalling, Jr.; foreword by Sally Quinn.
        p. cm.
        ISBN 0-8478-2024-6
        Mansions—Washington (D.C.)—Pictorial works. 2. Celebrities—
    Dwellings—Washington (D.C.)—Pictorial works. 3. Washington
    (D.C.)—Buildings, structures, etc.—Pictorial works.   I. Smalling, Jr., Walter.
    II. Title.
    NA7511.4.W37C54 1998
    728.8'09753   98-26054
                                                                      CIP

PRINTED IN ENGLAND

DESIGNED BY RENATO STANISIC

ACKNOWLEDGMENTS

✳

This book, like every other, depends on the good will, grace, and talent of many people. A study of privacy presents an interesting challenge, especially one that chronicles the private lives of public individuals. Patience, perseverance, persuasion, and countless conversations are required. Architecture in the home is among the most private of the arts, open to public view on the exterior and controlled privacy on the interior, as it should be. Many people are understandably reluctant to open their houses to the reading public, as well as to an architectural writer and photographer.

Our greatest debt and admiration go to the individuals whose houses, homes, and lives are portrayed in this book. They gave us access to their private realms, they answered our probing questions, they regaled us with wonderful and enlightening stories, and they graciously introduced us to others of like mind and heart. One patron paved the way for another friend, from Susan Mary Alsop, to Oatsie Charles, to Sally Quinn and Ben Bradlee, to Kate and Jim Lehrer, then Katharine Graham. We have tremendous respect for their commitment to the design and welfare of this city, and to creating interesting personal architectural environments in which to live. Others include: Darryl W. Carter; Olvia Demetriou and Theo Adamstein; John Dreyfuss and Mary Nobel Ours; George H. Eatman; Lee and Juliet C. Folger; Carl and Nancy Gewirz; Sam Gilliam and Annie Gawlack; Denyce Graves and David Perry; Kitty Kelley and John Zucker; Margot Kelly; Christopher and Deedy Ogden; David Schwarz, AIA; William and Lucinda Seale; Ambassador Andre and Lady Adam of Belgium; Ambassador and Lady Chrobog of the Republic of Germany; and former Ambassador and Lady Kerr of Great Britain.

Because so much of the book depended on trust, part of the process of creating the book included building the trust of people who did not know us. There were certain individuals who were particularly helpful in this regard. We depended dearly on their assistance and personal relationships as they introduced us to others while affirming our pursuit of architectural scholarship, including Washington, D.C., designer John Peters Irelan, and rare books dealer and designer Kinsey Marable. For introductions, arrangements, and access, we are also indebted to: David Beekum; Iris Broll, Chris Bluehdorn, and Anne Lange-Brennet of the German Embassy; Amy Caldwell of Tudor Place Foundation; Robert Culshaw and Amanda Downs of the British Embassy; Mary Drysdale, designer; Warren Eisenberg; Joan Fabry and Michael Sullivan; Judy A. Greenberg of The Kreeger Museum; Peter Harkness; Liz Hilton and Ev Small of Katharine Graham's office; Comer Jennings of Atlanta, Georgia; Norman Koontz, FAIA, and Alan Sandler of the American Architectural Foundation; Heather Lobdale of *Traditional Home*; Charles Lowe; David Mitchell, AIA; Mark Ohnmacht; Eryl Platzer of The

Octagon; Suzanne Stephens, Denyce Graves's assistant; Patricia Dane Rogers, Jura Konscious, and Kathy Legg of the *Washington Post*; and Gayle Rosenberg of *Architectural Digest*.

For archival materials and primary information, we are grateful to the following individuals: Nancy Edelman of Dumbarton House; Rex Scouten and Betty Monkman of the Office of the Curator, the White House; Ms. Kathleen Betts, curator of the Anderson House Museum; Neil W. Horstman of the White House Historical Association; William Seale, Historian of the White House; Hugh Newell Jacobson, FAIA, architect of the Ogden house; Cesar Pelli, FAIA, architect of the Gewirz house; Oswald Mathias Oswald, architect of the German Ambassador's residence; Judy Robinson and Joan Brierton of Robinson Associates; Sue A. Kohler of the Commission of Fine Arts and historian of Massachusetts Avenue; and Saskia Weinstein, New York–based designer.

We offer special thanks to Theo Adamstein of Chrome, Inc., who provided generous in-kind service on photographic processing.

To our friends and families, who selflessly offered us months and months of support and humored us with their interest as we told them endless tales about our escapades, go thanks, affection, and admiration. Their generosity extended to taking time to read text and edit photographs, to make personal calls on our behalf, and to talk through ideas as the book developed. We are blessed with friends who are smart and nice people. For Walter these include: Ray Rhinehart, Lisa Berg, Bill Courville, Jay Pagano, Heather Ewing, Doug Lakey, Bryan and Melissa Smalling Lakey, and Elsa Walsh; for Jan, these include Elizabeth Wainger, Meredith W. La Pier, Jean Bobrowske, Tom Leonhardt, Beth Dunlop, Bob Wilson, Peter Wiley, and Fred Starr. Mutual friends include William Murtagh, one of this country's founding fathers of preservation, and David Fram, the handsome, dark-haired man in the purple bathing suit.

Finally, to David Morton and Elizabeth White of Rizzoli go our thanks for encouraging us through the creation of this book. To Forrest MacCormack, our photographic assistant, we thank you for hundreds of hours of talent, hard work, and companionship. And to one another, we say thank you, for making this and many other things possible. Neither one of us could have come close to completing this book without the other, for knowledge of architecture and Washington, for talent, guidance, and mutual respect and encouragement.

Jan Cigliano
Walter Smalling, Jr.
Washington, D.C.

CONTENTS

FOREWORD

by Sally Quinn

✳

One day, shortly after Ben and I bought our house in Georgetown, I was standing in the empty entrance hallway looking out through the back door to the generous porch and garden beyond. It was a typical Washington summer day, sweltering and humid, and I was exhausted from having dealt with workmen and contractors since dawn. They had all left, it was twilight, and I was finally alone. I loved that time of day, when I could contemplate what we had done to the house and what I wanted to do, what I wanted the house to look and feel like.

I had a huge responsibility. This was a historic house, started in 1793 and completed in 1799 by a Scottish merchant named William Laird. George Washington was president at the time, Georgetown hardly existed, and the backyard ran all the way down to the Potomac. Later, it was owned and occupied by Abraham Lincoln's son Robert Todd Lincoln, and a number of distinguished residents. It was by all rights a museum, but it was also going to be my home. How was I to honor its history and still make it a cozy and livable place for our family and a comfortable and fun place for my friends?

I would muse every day about what life must have been like in the days when the house was first built, fantasizing about the people who lived there, what they wore, and what joys and sorrows they might have

Entry archway between the elliptical foyer and the main stair hall at the Octagon (page 55). The exquisitely articulated Regency detail was re-created during the 1990–95 restoration.

experienced so long ago. That particular day, tired, hot, and dusty, I leaned up against the door to the living room and closed my eyes, conjuring up former inhabitants of the house. I could almost hear them laughing, crying, singing, and shouting. I could even invent their stories: a carriage pulling up; the sound of horses' hooves; a man descending, barking orders to the driver, and racing up the front steps. My pulse quickened. Who was he? Why was he here? Was he bringing news of war or some political scandal? Was he here to propose marriage or to break off an engagement? An invitation to the White House? Was it someone's death? The president's perhaps?

It was then that I felt the presence of a woman at the back entrance to the hallway. Her fear was palpable and I could feel my own fear begin to match hers. My heart was racing. I opened my eyes and to my shock, there she was. She was actually standing before me, framed by the back doorway in the twilight, an eighteenth-century woman! She wore a white lace cap and a light-colored, full-skirted dress with a white bodice; soft brown curls surrounded her face. She was anxiously twisting her hands and seemed reluctant to come inside or offer a greeting. She didn't appear to register any notice of me.

I closed my eyes, thinking surely the light was playing tricks on me. When I opened them she was gone. Slowly, and with some trepidation, I walked to the back door and looked out on the porch. There was no sign of a human being. There was nobody in the garden, either.

I was overcome with chills, depite the evening torpor. Had I really seen a ghost, been transported back in time, or was it purely a figment of my fertile imagination?

Some weeks later I was visiting the Old Stone House on M Street, the oldest house in Georgetown and now a museum. It has a lovely garden that backs up to the alley across from our garden. The people who work there are historic interpreters, and dress in period costume. When I walked into the house I felt a shock of recognition. There was my eighteenth-century lady, in the exact dress I had seen her wear on my back porch that remarkable evening.

It seems she had seen our garden gate ajar when she was working in the Old Stone House garden and climbed the fence and crept in. She told me she was terribly nervous about trespassing but she walked up to the porch and peered into the darkened hallway nevertheless. Curious as she was, she felt an eerie chill, as though she, too, were in the presence of a ghost. She ran back down the steps and out of the gate. Despite her explanation, I still felt that the confluence that night of her presence and my own reverie had created more than just a fantasy and that I had actually glimpsed another life in another time.

All of this is to say that you cannot live in this city, particularly in Georgetown, without being constantly reminded of what went before you. There is history on every corner. I can't walk down a street without imagining who walked down that street one or two hundred years ago. I can't look out the window without seeing a house or a monument that reminds me of who was here before. From my office window as I write, I can see the Washington Monument, the Kennedy Center, Memorial Bridge, and Robert E. Lee's mansion. Just beyond the Washington Monument is the Capitol, and beyond the Kennedy Center is the Lincoln Memorial, the Jefferson Memorial, and the Vietnam Memorial. At Lee's mansion is Arlington Cemetery, and several miles down the road is Mount Vernon. I live only a few blocks away from the White House and Lafayette Square.

The architecture we live with is beautiful. A grand neoclassical, elegant Federal, or later Victorian is on every street, reflecting both the taste and political climate of their day.

Politics, Washington's main industry, pervades the city and imbues it with its personality. It seems that those with an interest in politics often choose a house that has some sort of political history. It's possible that George Washington visited our house; it is one of the few that were here during his presidency, and its owner was a prominent local figure. We have prints of George Washington all over the house as a reminder of when it was built. We have pictures of Lincoln, too, and of his son Robert when he lived here. One can only imagine the guests they had.

When I was decorating my house I felt I needed to walk a fine line between having it look and, more importantly, feel as though it were consistent with the architecture of its time, while also making it a house for today. Houses to me are living, changing things, and I did not want it to look or feel like a museum. It is always a terrible mistake to have them look as if the rooms should be roped off.

We have lots of antiques, most of them inherited from Ben's family. As is our house, they are all of the Federal period, which is my favorite period of design. For me, it represents the ultimate in simplicity, clean lines, and elegance. Nothing is more pleasing to me than a beautiful Federal house or piece of furniture. This doesn't mean that I don't have things from other periods—all of the upholstered furniture is modern, although the style is classic and traditional. I have oriental pieces that were popular during the Federal period, and some French and American country things as well.

In the end, though, the purposes of this house are comfort, ease, and pleasure. I'm always happy when I see my son Quinn's bike parked in the entrance hall, or his in-line skates or tennis racquet on the hall bench. Houses are to be lived in, added to, painted, redecorated, and renovated. They should reflect the people who live in them and the times in which they live. Most of all, they should evoke a sense of place. A Federal town house in Georgetown should not be decorated to look like a Malibu beach house or a Montana log cabin.

The Chinese concept of feng shui, a design principle that is currently popular in the West, advocates the importance of good vibrations and good feelings when entering a house. I can sense its absence immediately, and it is always for the same reasons. The owners or occupants have not been true to the character of the house. They have tried to distort its personality and style and design. Sometimes I have almost felt a house crying out, "Help me! Save me!" the minute I walk in the door. This is sadly true even in some of the wonderful historic Washington houses.

I'm an Army brat. I've lived all over the world. My family moved every year and a half and I ended up attending twenty-two schools. When you move that much you have to be attached to something. Fortunately, we had a very close family, but it was hard to make good friends in such a short time and then lose them. So I became attached to my houses. They became almost human to me, like friends, with names and personalities. Whenever we would leave a place I would tearfully go back into the house alone, just as we were about to drive away, and kiss the walls of each room, whispering, "Good-bye bedroom," "Good-bye dining room," "Good-bye living room," and finally, "Good-bye house." It was the most wrenching departure of all.

I've said my last good-bye to a house — in a pine box is how I'm leaving this one. This house is my friend, my companion, my refuge, my security. To many people it looks like an enormous, imposing, almost severe historic mansion. Not to me. The first time I saw the house, I walked down the alley to the back and pulled myself up over the fence so that I could see the old southern porch that runs the length of the house. Suddenly it was as if the house were crying out to me, "Sally, come save me!" I remember feeling tears well up in my eyes as I whispered, "Hello house." I had finally, after all these years, really come home.

✳

INTRODUCTION

✳

MOST OF OUR MEMORIES OF A BUILDING, A ROOM, OR A YARD EVOKE A PERSON OR AN OCCA-SION IN THE SETTING. OFTEN, IT SEEMS, WE REMEMBER CERTAIN AGES AND EVENTS IN OUR LIVES IN CONNECTION WITH A NEIGHBORHOOD, A STREET, A HOUSE, OR AN APARTMENT. AN ENDLESS STREAM OF ASSOCIATIONS AND FEELINGS IS ATTACHED TO A PLACE, AND ESPECIALLY TO A HOME.

THIS SENSE OF PLACE IS AT THE HEART OF *PRIVATE WASHINGTON*, A VISUAL PORTRAIT OF THE LIVING HISTORY OF TWENTY-SEVEN RESIDENCES IN WASHINGTON, D.C. SPANNING A PERIOD OF ABOUT TWO HUNDRED YEARS, FROM GEORGETOWN'S 1787 HALCYON HOUSE TO THE GERMAN AMBASSADOR'S residence of 1994, all the houses were created as private homes; four are now museums open to the public.

The homes in *Private Washington* are remarkable for their social, political, and personal memories, and for their artistic and architectural dimensions. Each residence bears the ancestry of individual patrons and family traditions, interweaving the private sanctuary of the family home with arenas for public display—rooms designed for the high purpose of the capital city.

Perhaps the most dramatic dichotomy between the private and the public is found in the eighteenth-century Halcyon House—now the home and studio of sculptor John Dreyfuss and photographer Mary Noble Ours (the house is occasionally also rented out for special entertaining to help finance its restoration). Benjamin Stoddert, first secretary of the navy, spent two years building this elegant Georgetown estate on land overlooking the Potomac River bluffs. Yet it took Dreyfuss two decades to rebuild the vast Georgian pile. The transition between private and public use is not always easy, yet several evenings each the neoclassical rooms are transformed for such luminaries as the Clintons, Madeleine Albright, or Dionne Warwick to dance the night away.

A CITY FOR RESIDENCE AND DESIGN

We can understand a lot about a place, a city like Washington, by the way residents have chosen to live and invest their money. The first message about Washington is that residence matters; The second is that design matters. Washington traditions honor a long history of conventional taste in architecture. The precedent began two centuries ago with George Washington, John Quincy Adams, Thomas Jefferson, and James Madison. General Washington may have been a military man by calling, but he was an international politician at heart. He had a vision for this city on the Potomac, an impulse that drew him to retain Major Pierre L'Enfant in 1791 to create a classical, monumental city of magnificent avenues, radials, boulevards, parks, and squares.

Washington's residential core developed slowly during the nineteenth century, expanding with the growth of government. Small neighborhoods on Capitol Hill, in Georgetown, and along Pennsylvania

Avenue west from the president's house amounted to a small town of only 640 houses in 1800; as late as 1842 Charles Dickens quipped that Washington was still merely "a city of magnificent intentions." Little building occurred during the Civil War, when Washington was turned into an armed camp of Union troops. Churches and large houses were used for hospitals and dirt roads were scarred by the constant passage of cannon wagons. Only after the war did a real residential city begin to take shape, thanks in large measure to the federal government and the unification of Georgetown, Washington City, and Washington County into one federal district. In 1871, Mayor Alexander R. ("Boss") Shepherd began a program of remarkable public works. He built the infrastructure, and paved, leveled, and landscaped streets. Although he may be notorious for his dubious accounting methods and unscrupulous business practices, Shepherd nevertheless can be credited with creating the public anatomy of a private Washington.

By the turn of the century, residential neighborhoods had expanded farther south toward the waterfront, and north and west along Seventh and Sixteenth streets and Connecticut Avenue. The pace of development accelerated after 1893 when Congress extended the original city boundaries beyond Florida Avenue north to Western Avenue at the Maryland line. The streetcar in the 1890s and then the automobile in the 1920s made it easier to live in the city's leafy, landscaped neighborhoods and commute to work downtown. Unlike other large American cities, in Washington, single-family homes predominate. Spurred by an expanding middle-income population, developers built volumes of houses in the outer subdivisions of Cleveland Park, the Palisades, Foxhall, Wesley Heights, Spring Valley, Massachusetts Heights, and along the Sixteenth Street corridor, solidifying the base of homeowners in the city.

While early-twentieth-century Washington presented a picture of happy times and healthy growth, the reality of a city dominated by politics, and by cultural tensions between the North and the South, as well as between black and white residents, could not help but prevail. Each segment of the community, however—political, social, affluent, middle-income, poor, black, white, Asian, Hispanic—left an indelible imprint on the shifting geography of the city's neighborhoods and architecture.

A CITY OF RESIDENCE

Over time and through consistent care, residents like those in *Private Washington*, among many others, people such as Thomas and Martha Custis Peter, Kathrine and John Folger, David Lloyd and Carmine Kreeger, Larz and Isabel Anderson, Katharine Graham, Chris and Deedy Ogden, Sam Gilliam and Annie Gawlack, have become as much institutional stewards of the city as are Washington's official emissaries and public agencies. They, and a much larger stable of those who regard Washington as their home, sustain the city's beauty and architectural integrity. They care for the public streets and parks, invest handsomely in its stock of houses and neighborhoods, and they invest their personal resources in the schools, libraries, playgrounds, and even firehouses to supplement inadequate city finances. We can also attribute Washington's strident and fairly successful land-use regulations—criticized by some for constituting a web of red tape of public approvals—to the citywide corps of vigilant Advisory Neighborhood Commissions and a wise Fine Arts Commission (established by Congress in 1910 to oversee the architectural development of all federal property in the District and Georgetown), as well as a universe of proactive residents loyal to their town and neighbors. For the extent of the city's external function to national society and the international community, residents historically remain committed to the "home" city, as much as they do to their own neighborhood enclave. Like any other American town, village, or city, Washington remains a community supported by the culture of the people who live here over the long term.

ARCHITECTURAL CONVENTIONS

Pierre L'Enfant shared, if not surpassed, George Washington's vision of grandeur for this capital. But L'Enfant tended toward the grandiose, and he believed he was subject only to the president's authority and ignored the commissioners (he certainly thought nothing of their competence). For his hauteur, President Washington fired him in 1792, only a year into his work, yet to the French designer's good fortune—and that of future residents—his associates, surveyor Andrew Ellicott and engineer Benjamin Banneker, stepped in to map out L'Enfant's Plan of Washington for the ten-square-mile territory.

L'Enfant's grand urban design of tree-lined boulevards and radials called for classical architecture for the young city's largest buildings, defined by Renaissance- and Roman-inspired columns and friezes. From 1783 until the end of the Civil War, only architects with solid classical backgrounds held the position of Architect of the Capitol, the high-level public servant who oversaw all federal building projects and who was the leading architectural voice in Washington.

By the early 1800s, even residential architecture was influenced by classical tastes, and the Georgian, Federal, and Regency styles emerged prominently. High standards of design matured in this semi-tropical wasteland, where large, lone, monumental residences, like the Tayloes' Octagon or the Peters' Tudor Place, stood out to signal conventional standards.

Washingtonians have always tended to be conservative in their architectural tastes, followers of national trends rather than innovators. In step with national fashion, Romantic design influences emerged around mid-century when Andrew Jackson Downing's landscapes for the Smithsonian Institution and the White House grounds, and James Renwick's great Smithsonian Gothic castle swayed local preferences toward medieval and Italianate revival influences. The most fashionable residences of this era arose on Georgetown Hill, today the homes of Marion Oats ("Oatsie") Charles and Katharine Graham.

The Romantic movement lasted through the end of the nineteenth century, when the age of eclectic energy in architecture came to a quiet close as all things classical re-emerged around 1900, in step with the rise of European academic styles and the widespread influence of the Ecole des Beaux-Arts in Paris. Some of Washington's finest buildings came out of this era, notably Larz and Isabel Anderson's 1905 limestone mansion on Massachusetts Avenue, designed for the Massachusetts natives by Boston architects Little & Browne; Sir Edwin Landseer Lutyens's 1928 masterpiece for the British ambassador's residence; and John Russell Pope's last residence, for John and Kathrine Folger in 1935–36, completed as Pope was finishing work on the National Gallery of Art.

Contemporary architects who have designed buildings in Washington have tended to exercise their most conventional impulses, even such avant-garde designers as Michael Graves and Marcel Breuer. This is what Washington patrons want, so it is no surprise that many of the century's leading architects—Philip Johnson, I. M. Pei, Frank Lloyd Wright, Cesar Pelli, Walter Gropius, Richard Neutra—have designed only one residence in this international capital of art and culture, and such greats as Frank Gehry, Charles Gwathmey and Richard Meier have designed none.

A CITY OF DESIGN

Early on, the White House, begun in 1797 and occupied in 1800, set the cultural tone of the town. Its first occupant was John Adams, followed by Thomas Jefferson (who had secretly submitted an anonymous design for the White House competition, but did not win; builder-architect James Hoban did). It is the national capital's great good fortune that the beautiful city designed and developed by its chief stewards has been sustained for more than two hundred years by certain presidents and congressmen and residents.

In 1901, Senate District Committee chairman,

Senator James McMillan, inspired by the classical grandeur of the World's Columbian Exposition of 1893, created the McMillan Plan Commission to restore and maintain the formal design of Pierre L'Enfant's original plan. The blue-ribbon McMillan commissioners—Daniel H. Burnham, who led the Columbian Exposition's design team, and his colleagues Frederick Law Olmsted Jr. (son of the great landscape designer who created the Capitol grounds), Charles Follen McKim, and sculptor Augustus Saint-Gaudens—established enforceable guidelines for implementing L'Enfant's scheme and for regulating architectural design on federal property. Quite importantly, they also reaffirmed academic classicism as the aesthetic model for Washington's buildings—whether institutional, commercial, or residential. During the 1930s and early 1940s, Franklin Delano Roosevelt sponsored the building of huge federal offices, monuments, and museums along the Mall, masterpieces that reinforced the classical ethos. Finally, in the early 1960s, John F. Kennedy was the last twentieth-century president to bear a measurable influence on Washington design and development through major building projects of the Pennsylvania Avenue Development Corporation, which Senator Patrick Moynihan oversaw through its completion in the 1990s. Thus, even in this most democratic of towns, the presence of national leaders who value intelligent design have lent credence to an environment of high architectural standards.

ARCHITECTURAL PATRONAGE

In the late eighteenth century, when the city was founded, the notion of the house as a work of art was limited to the rarefied stratosphere of The Octagon, Tudor Place, or Halcyon House. For patrons, an architect-designed house on one of the best streets affirmed a family's social and financial standing, and, in this city, its political relevance. The Townsends and Andersons on Massachusetts Avenue, the Whites and Laughlins in the Meridian Hill neighbor-

hood, and the Frasers on Connecticut Avenue made a sizable investment in ensuring their status by the craftsmanship of the house they built. By the same token, such architects as Joseph Hornblower and his partner James Marshall, Waddy B. Wood, Henri de Sibour, and George Oakley Totten prospered in the society of their affluent clients. Patrons reinforced the prestige of their architects, and architects promoted the stature of their patrons during this period, roughly between 1890 and 1930.

Yet patronage houses became increasingly rare as the twentieth century progressed. By the 1990s, hiring an architect was as rare as it had been in the 1790s. Such practical matters as cost, time, and resale value became deterrents for many wealthy individuals. Those who did commission architect-designed residences were often motivated by reasons more philosophically compelling than practical. The notion of investment architecture—the residence as a work of art and the patron as the collector—moved the Gewirzes, for instance, who are professional art collectors, to retain Cesar Pelli to design their house.

The people in this book tend to be quite public and proud in most arenas, while they fiercely guard the private domains of their personal residences. Many who agreed to appear did so reluctantly and after long deliberation. Others declined for several reasons, some because of a longing to preserve anonymity in at least one part of their lives, some because their public service positions preclude displays of elegant living.

The Georgetown estate of Katharine Graham, chief steward of the *Washington Post* publishing empire and acclaimed author, enforces her stature while serving her personal needs for comfort and unguarded times with family and friends. We also find, in moving beyond the exterior architecture of walls and windows and roof eaves of this house and others, an intriguing interior architecture that reveals great creativity, such as Cesar Pelli's sunlit long gallery in the Gewirz house or Hugh Jacobsen's glass-walled orangerie in the Ogden house. Here are the best surprises.

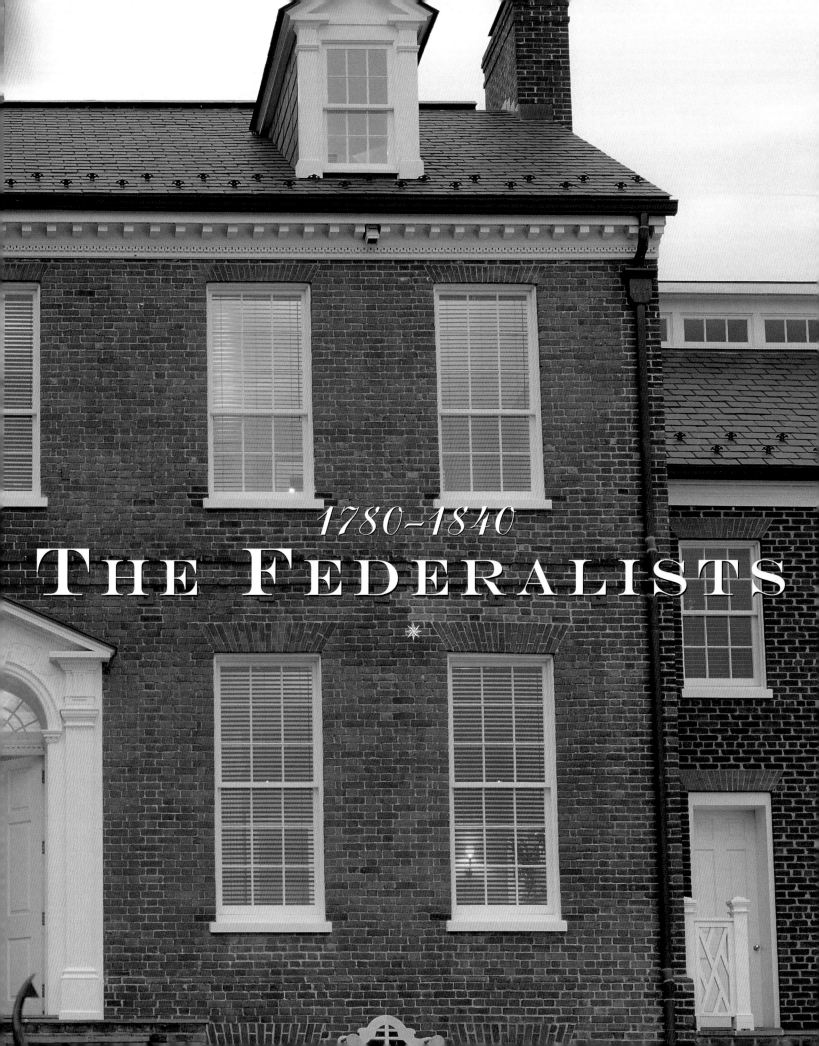

1780–1840
The Federalists

HALCYON HOUSE

1787 | *Architect Unknown*
Restored **1978–97** | *John Dreyfuss and George Stravropoulos*

*In the late eighteenth
century, the generously
proportioned rooms of
Halcyon House welcomed
such leading citizens of the
young nation as George
Washington, Thomas
Jefferson, and John Adams.
John Dreyfuss and his wife,
Mary Noble Ours (above)
restored Halcyon
House from 1978 to 1997.*

WITH THE POWER TO CALM OCEAN WAVES, THE FABLED BIRD OF THE ANCIENTS SEEMS AN APPROPRIATE NAMESAKE FOR HALCYON HOUSE. INDEED, THIS HOUSE HAS NOT ONLY GRACED, BUT ENDURED THE LIVES OF MULTIPLE OWNERS AND OCCUPANTS, FROM BENJAMIN AND REBECCA STODDERT, WHO BUILT IT IN THE EARLY 1800S, TO THE DERANGED ALBERT CLEMENS, WHO DIS-FIGURED THE HOUSE FOR FORTY YEARS IN THE EARLY TWENTIETH CENTURY. ONGOING DECAY AND PIECEMEAL REMODELING AS THE GREAT MANSION'S FOOTINGS SHIFTED SLOWLY DOWN GEORGETOWN HILL SEEMED THE FATE OF HAL-CYON HOUSE UNTIL 1978, WHEN JOHN DREY-FUSS SAW IT THROUGH A REBIRTH.

The reception hall opens into the large kitchen, which is designed to accommodate both catering for large groups and private dinners for two.

Two centuries ago, prospering shipping merchant Benjamin Stoddert chose the elevated Prospect Hill site so that he could monitor ships coming into port and watch the Potomac's tides winding south from Great Falls to the open waters of the Tidewater region. Stoddert looked out on a panorama of untamed shores and clear waters, a view then unobstructed by concrete bridges and high rises on the Virginia skyline. The few years he had previously spent in Philadelphia, apprenticing in the shipping trade and then serving under John Adams as secretary of the Revolutionary War Board, impressed him with the finery of the Georgian style houses around Rittenhouse Square. Now he advertised his own affluence on a prominent site above the seaport that had made him wealthy, styling Halcyon House "after the manner of some of the elegant houses I have seen in Philadelphia."

In details and materials, the house is very similar to those in Philadelphia. Yet, where those houses are typically attached and four stories high, Halcyon

House stands free from all others on the block and rises only two stories. The grandeur of design, along with a gracious, pedimented entry that leads to a formal central hall rather than to a side hall, is more akin to the houses in Philadelphia's Fairmont Park than to those around Rittenhouse Square. The red-brick construction highlighted by a mid-level string course and the white, finely articulated classical detailing, however, suggest the finest qualities of the Georgian.

With its Georgetown address, Halcyon House became a convenient meeting place for the close society of General Washington, John Adams, and Thomas Jefferson, among others. By 1840, the Stodderts had left the homestead and new generations of owners occupied it through the 1890s. The turn of the twentieth century marked the onset of an ominous era for Halcyon House, when the nephew of Samuel Clemens (Mark Twain) took over. Known to be "touched," secretive, and obsessive, Albert Clemens believed he would live as long as he continued to build in the house. He added the two-story wings to either side of the main section, and encased the original Georgian structure in a four-story, neo-Palladian shell. The exterior defacement, as some claimed

The pool terrace affords spectacular views of the Francis Scott Key Bridge and the Rosslyn, Virginia, skyline beyond.

it was, matched the extent of Clemens's interior alterations. He created hundreds of nonfunctional spaces: doors that led to walls, rooms not large enough to stand in, hallways and stairs circling around to hallways and stairs. He walked about town in a torn coat and rumpled trousers, seemingly content enough to remain separated from his wealthy wife, enjoying the creativity and company of one of his carpenters, with whom he lived in the basement. The estranged Mrs. Elizabeth White Clemens, daughter of Senator White from New Hampshire, was equally happy to send Clemens money "on condition that he stay away from her," a Washington *Times-Herald* reporter wrote in 1952. And so he did. With doors padlocked, Clemens continued to build onto Halcyon House until his death in 1938.

Future owners included the Sterling family in the 1940s, Anne and George Gray in the 1950s, Georgetown University for a brief time in the 1960s, and Edmund Dreyfuss's development partnership in 1966, which tried and failed for twelve years to redevelop Halcyon House into a commercial venture. One scheme after another was rejected by the Fine Arts Commission, which held that Halcyon House possessed too much historic significance to undergo dramatic changes that might lessen its integrity.

Enter twenty-eight-year-old John Dreyfuss, Edmund's son, who returned to Washington and began showing Halcyon House to prospective developers when his father suffered an incapacitating stroke in 1978. Edmund Dreyfuss died in 1982, the same year the National Trust turned down Dreyfuss's proposal to accept Halcyon House as a gift because it would not be possible to maintain the house as a museum without a sustaining endowment. With few options remaining, John Dreyfuss and other family members collectively agreed to undertake the massive project of restoring the house.

Nine years of construction encompassed a ten-thousand-square-foot excavation—opening up the ground behind and under the house to put in the equivalent of three floors of concrete retaining walls—and the restoration of the graceful Georgian rooms to their pre-Clemens condition. The structural foundation doubles as the walls for Dreyfuss's massive, below-grade sculpture studio, brilliantly lighted by floor-to-ceiling French doors opening to the rear driveway and a clerestory gable that peaks up into the terraced garden above.

"The minute the restoration was finished," says Dreyfuss, "the incredibly fragile historic house began to deteriorate again." Maintenance over the years, and from day to day, is critical in sustaining this eighteenth-century cultural treasure. "If it is not impeccably maintained," he says, "I will have hell to pay." To whom he doesn't say. But more than one individual's promise seems to underpin the commitment to Halcyon House—the community, standards of architectural integrity, and Washington tradition are ever present.

BEN BRADLEE & SALLY QUINN HOUSE

1798 | *Builder–Architect Unknown*

The parlor satisfies Ben Bradlee's requirement that rooms must be at once intimate and grand. Throughout the house, rooms are "big when you need them to be and small when you don't," he says.

IN THE EARLY 1980S, BEN BRADLEE AND SALLY QUINN HAD BEEN MARRIED FOUR YEARS AND WERE HAPPILY LIVING IN A DUPONT CIRCLE TOWN HOUSE DESIGNED BY WASHINGTON ARCHITECT WADDY B. WOOD. BEN COULD ENVISION LIVING THE REST OF HIS LIFE IN THIS HOUSE, SO CONTENT AND COMFORTABLE WERE HE AND SALLY. BEN HAS LIVED IN MANY PLACES THROUGHOUT HIS JOURNALIST'S LIFE, THE LAST FOUR DECADES IN GEORGETOWN, CHEVY CHASE, AND A NUMBER OF EUROPEAN CITIES. HIS WIFE, BY CONTRAST, WHO GREW UP IN A MILITARY FAMILY AND WAS ACCUSTOMED TO MOVING EVERY TWO YEARS, INDULGES HER TALENT FOR INTERIOR DESIGN BY BUYING AND

renovating historic houses. When their son Quinn was born in 1982, Ben completely revised his thinking about staying put in their modest-sized house and Sally savored the chance to restore yet another one.

"We were your slightly atypical working couple," Ben says, remembering their search, he the executive editor of the *Washington Post*, and she a national journalist and author. They needed a house to accommodate a family of three, a quiet writing place for two authors, the occasional large-scale party, and frequent intimate dinners with friends. They found the perfect house, a central-hall Federal residence on coveted N Street in Georgetown, expensive but an eighteenth-century beauty.

Two centuries ago, Scottish shipping and tobacco merchant John Laird had built this three-story brick residence. The original 1798 house comprised only the central three-bay section with the raised fanlight doorway at the eastern end. The shipper's landed estate covered acres and acres of this small village, reaching all the way down to the Potomac riverfront, where Mr. Laird looked out over his cows, sheep, and hogs grazing on the lawn of Georgetown's commercial port. He bequeathed the house to his daughter, Margaret, who treasured living here with her aunt, Elizabeth Dick. Miss Peggy and Miss Betsy, as they were known, were beloved figures in their stately residence. In time, an elderly Peggy gave the house to her younger sister, Barbara, who had

The center hall leads from the front door to the rear porch and garden, opening onto the grand double parlor (opposite) and other public rooms and creating a country house feeling. Upstairs, the profusion of objects and mementos on Sally Quinn's desk (above) reveals her myriad enthusiasms.

*The master bedroom
provides a quiet refuge with
a sweeping view of the
garden and the Potomac
River beyond.*

A fresh palette of soft blues and yellows makes the dining room at once formal and intimate. Blue-and-white Cantonese porcelain plates, Bradlee family heirlooms, line the walls.

married James Dunlop, Jr. (the law partner of Francis Scott Key and later Chief Justice of the Supreme Court of the District of Columbia). An appropriate residence for this prominent couple, the mansion would become a welcome retreat for Justice Dunlop years later. During the Civil War his judicial career was cut short, when, as a native Southerner he remained sympathetic to the Confederate Army (a loyalty shared by many of his Georgetown neighbors), and President Lincoln swiftly removed him from the bench. The Dunlops lived out their lives in grand style in this Georgetown house, the retired justice thriving as a prosperous lawyer.

After his death in 1915, in what seems a bittersweet irony today, his widow, Barbara Laird Dunlop, sold the family home to the eldest son of her husband's nemesis, Robert Todd Lincoln. The Lincolns continued to amass property to either side of the house along N Street; Robert's widow later built an attached brick town house on the west for her two unmarried daughters, an extension that amplifies the house's horizontal breadth while reflecting the wide sweep of the backyard property. (With connecting doorways hidden deep in the current owners' closets, the attached house is now a rental.)

This eighteen-room, three-story house (plus basement and attic) is large, to be sure, though it does not overwhelm. It is the natural human scale, each room squarely proportioned floor to ceiling, and the breezy cross-circulation front to back that reminds one of a classic yet perfectly charming country house. The rooms, Ben remarks, "are big when you need them to be and small when you don't." The verandah-style porch steps down to a pool, tennis court, and a backyard with leafy trees and a green lawn. Stretching the width of the main house is a long gallery in the best Southern tradition, looking out onto the landscape.

Sally works out of the house most days, juggling television and journalistic assignments, promoting her latest book, writing in her sunny third-floor office, and devoting precious time to Quinn. Across the hall, her husband's study is filled with paperwork from the *Post*, where he still spends many a day as vice-president-at-large.

Downstairs, the rose-colored double living room is accented by a fresh palette of fabrics in garden colors, and a rich collection of books and art. The museum-like dining room is decorated in soft blues and yellows, making it appear more intimate than formal. The walls are lined with the blue Canton porcelain plates that Ben inherited from his nineteenth-century ancestors, shipping merchants in the China trade.

"I feel like a caretaker," Sally Quinn emphasizes. "This is an incredibly gorgeous Federal house and I wanted the classicism to come through and to still feel comfortable." Indeed, the Bradlee-Quinns' respect for the heritage of this structure is matched only by their impeccable care and flattering design.

THE OCTAGON

1797-1801 | Dr. William Thornton

It was a politically savvy George Washington who in 1797 persuaded his friend and fellow Virginian, twenty-nine-year-old Colonel John Tayloe of Mount Airy, to build his stately city house two blocks west of the White House, which was then under construction. Washington had recently been chosen as the capital of the young nation by the president's constitutional colleagues, a choice the commander-in-chief thoroughly endorsed on the merits of the territory's proximity to his Virginia estate at Mount Vernon and for its natural advantages between North and South on the Potomac River. Although Colonel

During the War of 1812, The Octagon provided a refuge to President James Madison and his wife, Dolley, after the British burned the White House. These inner doors were added by President Madison to separate the public foyer from the private living spaces beyond.

Tayloe, Virginia's largest plantation, had earlier favored building his urban residence in Philadelphia, President Washington convinced his friend of the capital's bright future. Tayloe acquired a triangular lot at the corner of New York Avenue and Eighteenth Street in April 1797, a site visible to all entering the city from the Virginia country, especially to those approaching the president's house.

To assure his satisfaction with the design of the residence, Tayloe asked two premier architects to prepare preliminary drawings: Dr. William Thornton, first architect of the U.S. Capitol building, and his arch rival, Benjamin Henry Latrobe, Thornton's successor in 1803 as architect of the Capitol. (With President Jefferson's blessing, Latrobe later altered Thornton's original design.) Tayloe selected Thornton, his choice ostensibly based on the architect's Federal-style design. Yet one cannot overlook the camaraderie shared by patron and architect over their love for horse racing. Indeed, one suspects that their mutual enthusiasm for horses, politics, and friends George Washington, James Madison, Thomas Jefferson, John Adams, and James Monroe also contributed to their rewarding architectural collaboration.

William Thornton was a Renaissance man in the best sense. Not only did he greatly influence federal design in Washington, he also made his mark in the history books as inventor, with Robert Fulton, of the steam boat. Born in the West Indies in 1761, Thornton was educated in medicine at Edinburgh. He went on to Paris to study drawing and painting with the French masters, arriving in the new America in 1787 — New York City to Wilmington and Philadelphia, then Washington. Throughout his life, he pursued many careers — in architecture, medicine, philosophy, finance, insurance, astronomy, botany, poetry, painting, and sheep and horse breeding. His love for invention was so great that he served as the first U.S. Patent Commissioner.

Why the Tayloes named their residence The Octagon remains a mystery to this day. The slightly elongated six-sided plan fronted by a semicircular projection is surely a distinctive feature, designed to emphasize the site's prominent triangular intersection. The architect ingeniously adjusted the strict rectilinearity of traditional Regency design to adapt to the triangular lot, creating an innovative hexagonal building filled with natural light and interesting spatial dimensions, a plan on a par with Thomas Jefferson's residences at Poplar Forest and Monticello in Virginia and Dr. Thornton's design for the Peter family at Tudor Place in Georgetown (see page 45). As a work of early American architecture, The Octagon appears avant-garde even to a late-twentieth-century eye. Basic design elements are emphasized: spatial flows and visual vistas across rooms and public areas, a reductionist ornamental scheme centering on the dramatic play of light against color contrasts and unusual room dimensions and shapes combining the geometries of a circle, two rectangles, and a triangle.

The raised entry porch opens onto a perfectly circular vestibule, painted in its original bright turquoise and pink colors; the broad door and large windows are crafted to conform to the room's circular shape. The exterior is executed in muted red brick and trimmed with creamy Aquia Creek sandstone and white marble panels over the second-floor windows. The vertical emphasis of the raised entrance portico with Doric columns strengthens the house's stature. Typical of the period—and of the Tayloes' affluence—public spaces occupy the two first-floor rooms. Hand-crafted details adorn the hardwood mahogany

The dramatic and graceful stairway winds up three floors, with large northeast-facing windows filling the stairwell with light.

doors and an acanthus motif is engraved in brass doorknobs. The sculpted stone fireplace mantel in the drawing room was shipped from London in 1799. The prized mantel drew the attention of New York architect Stanford White when, as the then secretary of the American Institute of Architects, he sought to buy it from the Tayloe family for the house he was designing for Mrs. Leland Stanford. The Tayloe heirs declined White's request to remove the room's central feature.

For two hundred years, The Octagon's stature has always been identified with that of the Tayloes. In early-nineteenth-century Washington, they represented the joining of Maryland's and Virginia's two leading families: Ann Ogle Tayloe was the daughter of Maryland governor Benjamin Ogle, and John Tayloe was heir to Virginia's three-thousand-acre Mount Airy. John Tayloe, who owned more than five hundred slaves in town and on his plantation, enjoyed his prominence as a friend of presidents,

Incorporating circles, rectangles, and triangles in rooms of unusual dimensions, the design of The Octagon was avant-garde in 1797 and remains so today. The house was built to impress, and every detail attested to the stature of the Tayloe family. Even the vivid color scheme was a sign of wealth; only a rich man could afford such expensive pigments in the eighteenth century.

statesmen, and diplomats. Ann Tayloe entertained frequently in The Octagon's dining and drawing rooms with afternoon receptions, evening balls, and dinner parties. Georgetown's leading families topped the Tayloes' guest lists, as did the town's political bright lights. While John Tayloe's civic engagements helped to establish St. John's Parish at Lafayette Square and the Branch Bank of the United States, his greatest pleasure was the Washington Jockey Club, where he served as president and grand master of the town's horse racing, the most popular of all public amusements.

Yet the Tayloe household was not without tragedy, and, as legend tells it, The Octagon is haunted by the ghost of the Tayloes' daughter. The girl allegedly threw herself to her death down the great spiral staircase when her staunchly Federalist father refused to let her marry a young Englishman. Some claim that her ethereal vision, fueled by grief and despair of unrequited love, wafts in the glow of candlelight.

Even with this, the glory of The Octagon's heyday endures, the most spectacular year occurring early on in the house's history, in 1814–15, when it was used as the wartime White House of President James Madison and his wife, Dolly, after British troops burned the White House, and much of the city, on August 24, 1814. It was here, in the second-floor Round Room, now the Treaty Room, on February 17, 1815, that President Madison ratified the Treaty of Peace with Great Britain, at long last restoring peace in America. The Tayloes lived out their lives in The Octagon, Colonel Tayloe until 1828, and Mrs. Tayloe until 1855.

Tayloe heirs owned the house until the turn of the century, renting it to institutional occupants in keeping with the neighborhood's changing character. A military hospital occupied the house during the Civil War, as was the case with many large manses in Washington. In 1865, a Catholic girls' school, St. Rose's Technical Institute, moved in, followed in 1866 by the U.S. government's Hydrographic Office. In 1879, the Tayloe heirs apparently felt no bonds with the old residence and subdivided it into a dozen studio apartments. After twenty years of decay, the American Institute of Architects rescued the landmark in 1899, when it rented, renovated, and occupied it for its national headquarters. The Institute finally bought the house from the Tayloe family in 1902.

Yet even with this conviction to save the historic landmark, the AIA seemed to threaten its own stewardly reputation in the mid-1960s when it began planning to build a new AIA headquarters behind (and overshadowing) The Octagon—a contemporary, seven-story, glass-and-steel backdrop to the historic residence. Outcries filled the editorial pages of the local and national press, accusing the central body of America's architects of "historic desecration." Historians, preservationists, and even some architects were incensed by the grossly modern office building juxtaposed against this refined Federal mansion,

wondering how the same organization that had saved The Octagon in 1902 could now destroy its modest-scaled setting. In the end, the AIA acquiesced and dismissed the original architects chosen to design the headquarters. The Cambridge Design Collective was then hired to work with the Institute to create a design-by-committee building, ostensibly one that defers to The Octagon.

While the most severe critics have not wavered in their belief that the design and scale of the headquarters is inappropriate to the Octagon grounds, the AIA's century of stewardship suggests that the Institute and the American Architectural Foundation (the AIA's non-profit partner, which took over as owner in 1964) have dedicated substantial resources to stabilize, renovate, and restore The Octagon. They reinforced the first two floors in 1947–49, restored the kitchen, installed central heating and air conditioning, and reproduced the front door fanlight in 1968–70. The most extensive restoration, in 1990–95, encompassed an archaeological excavation of the basement and a complete restoration of the interior rooms and exterior walls and surfaces—an undertaking that has at last returned the patina of stately elegance to this residence.

MARGOT KELLY HOUSE

c.1798–1800 | *Builder Unknown*

Built around 1800, when Capitol Hill was still a collection of rustic dirt roads, Margot Kelly's house was very much in scale with its neighbors. Over the years, the area deteriorated, but recently it has been significantly revitalized. Kelly has been active in that process through restoration of several other residential and commercial properties.

WHEN A TRADESMAN BUILT THIS CHARMING GREEK REVIVAL FARMHOUSE ON CAPITOL HILL, AROUND 1800, THE FEDERAL GOVERNMENT HAD ONLY RECENTLY RELOCATED TO WASHINGTON, D.C., FROM NEW YORK CITY. THE HOUSE ROSE AMID A RUSTIC COMMUNITY OF DIRT ROADS, STOREFRONT SHOPS, AND FRAME AND BRICK TOWN AND ROW HOUSES. CIVIL SERVANTS AND BUILDING CREWS WORKING ON THE CONSTRUCTION OF THE NEW CAPITOL OCCUPIED THE MODEST DWELLINGS, WHILE BOARDING HOUSES ACCOMMODATED TRANSIENT CONGRESSMEN WHEN THEY CAME TO TOWN. THIS SMALL HOUSE AT THE CORNER OF A AND THIRD STREETS WAS VERY MUCH IN KEEPING WITH THE SCALE OF THE

The living room was part of the original house. Early in the nineteenth century, the library and dining room were added to the west, along with a full second floor and the present handsome Greek revival entrance porch.

neighborhood in the early years of the capital city; neither Charles Bulfinch's dome (1822–24) nor the monumental Library of Congress next door yet existed. Today, although Margot Kelly's two-story residence appears petite in the shadow of its imposing stone and marble neighbors, it is a remarkable testimony to the endurance of Capitol Hill's residential life that this small, freestanding house stands well preserved in what has become a densely institutionalized neighborhood.

Ms. Kelly, a native of Düsseldorf, Germany, arrived in the United States in 1950 as a diplomat with the newly opened West German embassy. In 1966 she bought this house from the estate of the deceased owner, who had lived here for sixty years. The single-family residence had been on the market for months, located as it was in the then deteriorated Capitol Hill neighborhood.

Yet Kelly was as confident then as she is today about two things: the neighborhood's merits and investing in undervalued property. This is her mien. Twice married and divorced, and having left the embassy in 1955, she focused her attentions on real estate brokerage and investment. She began buying, renovating, and selling little houses in the Burleith and Georgetown neighborhoods of northwest Washington, one by one. It was her panacea in the face of life's vicissitudes, she says, "rather than see a psychiatrist, as many of my friends did, I painted doors." In 1964, she decided to seize what she saw as ripe opportunities in the fledgling district of southeast Washington, a neighborhood that appealed to her investment acumen as well as her passion for community development. She bought this stuccoed brick house for her home within the year, and also acquired an early-twentieth-century commercial building on Eighth and G streets for redevelopment. Ever since, she has made it her mission to revitalize the neighborhood.

Margot approached the renovation of her residence as she does all other projects, by retaining loyal and quality craftsmen, and taking deliberate care with every detail, regardless of the extra time or cost that might entail.

"If you do things right in the first place," she remarks about the house's

superb condition more than thirty years after the renovation, "they will last."
The underground cellar foundation and the structural framing suggest that
the builder constructed the house on a sidehall floor plan, the living space
comprised of the eastern side of the present center hall, and including a living parlor and a kitchen with a large fireplace, and perhaps sleeping rooms
upstairs (the full second floor appears to be a later addition). The house was
then enlarged during the early decades of the nineteenth century, perhaps by
the family that built the house. The addition included a small library and dining room on the west side of the central hall, and the stylish Greek revival
front porch with fluted Doric columns. Typical of many vernacular-styled
houses built along the eastern seaboard during this period, the Kelly house
retains the low, seven-and-a-half-foot ceilings and six-and-a-half-foot doorways trimmed with bull's-eye molding.

Kelly enjoys a good deal of privacy in what is today a fairly congested
location around the Library of Congress, the Shakespeare Library, several
large churches, and the Pennsylvania Avenue commercial district one block
away. The biggest surprise is the secret garden patio on the side of the house,
sheltered partially by a two-story verandah and
protected from city noises by a barrier of wooden
trellises and healthy thickets of vines and bushes.

Having lived in war-ravaged Berlin before
coming to the United States, Margot Kelly had
developed the vision to see beyond crumbling
buildings and vagrants on the streets, to a site's
inherent vitality. Here, she finds it along Eighth
Street's retail block, a main street of sorts lined
with turn-of-the-century buildings (known locally
as Barracks Row, across from the U.S. Marine
Barracks). When she started buying the five commercial buildings she now owns in the 700 block
of Eighth Street, they were tenanted by a bowery
of pawns shops, liquor stores, and bars. Her efforts
to renovate this area required more than faith and
hope; it also called for money, experience, and her
personal commitment, a commitment she has sustained on the board of the Barracks Row Business
Alliance and the Capitol Hill Association of Merchants & Professionals. A charming and witty
woman whose soft beauty belies her age, Margot
Kelly stands out as a sparkling entrepreneurial
spirit anchoring the community.

*Despite the proximity of
the public buildings of Capitol
Hill, this garden remains
private and secret.*

TUDOR PLACE

1805–16 | *Dr. William Thornton*

The elegant proportions and Federal detailing of the dining room are the work of Dr. William Thornton, architect of the Capitol and The Octagon. Considered one of the finest houses in America and certainly the finest Georgian estate in Washington, Tudor Place was owned continuously for nearly two centuries by the Peter family.

In the Georgetown of 1807, Tudor Place, with its prominent architecture, pastoral setting, and formal gardens, was the finest Georgian estate in the city. Considering the stability of its continuous ownership by the Peter family for nearly two centuries, Tudor Place is a site that has witnessed many turning points in its time—in the lives of five generations of Peters, and in the surrounding lives of a city and a nation. When wealthy landowner Thomas Peter and his wife, Martha Parke Custis Peter, acquired Tudor Place in 1805, they settled in the most rural (and the highest) part of Georgetown, which had been

The parlor (above) and the more formal drawing room (opposite) are furnished with Peter family heirlooms, including a number of pieces from Mount Vernon bequeathed to Martha Parke Custis Peter by her grandmother Martha Washington.

founded as an independent city in 1751. Scarce few were either rich or pioneering enough to settle on land north of Dumbarton Street; most shippers, merchants, and residents built warehouses and town houses around the canal and the prosperous port, creating a dense settlement around Water and M streets. The Peters' property covered the entire block bounded by Q and R, Thirty-first and Thirty-second streets, truly rustic territory of wooded stands and dirt roads; the closest neighbors were four blocks east, at Evermay.

It seems certain that the Peters purchased Tudor Place with a vision of their residential property, and perhaps even their neighborhood. The grounds had been partially developed in 1794 by tobacco exporter Francis Lowndes, who began building the west and east wings of an unfinished mansion. When the Peters bought the house they and their eight children moved into the west wing and turned the east wing into a stable and carriage house. The young Mrs. Peter was best known at the time as one of the four beautiful granddaughters of former First Lady Martha Washington. She brought to her marriage a generous inheritance from her grandparents and a family tradition for commissioning fine

architecture. Her sister and brother-in-law, Eliza and Thomas Law, had recently retained the leading architect of federal Washington, Dr. William Thornton, to design and build their Capitol Hill residence. So pleased with the results, and with Thornton's friendly manner, Eliza introduced the architect to the Peters. Thornton melded easily with the fashionable set, having arrived first in Philadelphia from Paris and Edinburgh, where he was an intimate of Benjamin Franklin, and then George Washington in 1793 when he was chosen to be the first architect of the Capitol building. Thornton had also recently completed The Octagon in 1801 for the John Tayloes.

For the Peters, Thornton designed a Georgian style mansion that combined large-scale and delicate proportions, a house that faces the high south lawn in perfect symmetry, overlooking Q Street and Georgetown Harbor. From the main entrance on the north garden side, one passes through the open-air salon with drawing room and parlor to either side, and is drawn through to the domed circular porch on the south, which is faced with floor-to-ceiling sliding glass windows.

Mr. and Mrs. Peter opened their home to presidents and foreign heads of state, welcoming an elderly Marquis de Lafayette for tea in 1824 and a defeated General Robert E. Lee for sherry (and whiskey) in 1869. Thomas and Martha Peter, their five sons, and three daughters America, Columbia, and Britannia remained unwavering Union and abolitionist loyalists. Yet they were willful pacifists throughout the Civil War: while the Peters resided in the North, they kept close family ties with the Custis family, who were deeply rooted in Southern loyalties.

The widowed Mrs. Peter bequeathed her residence to her youngest child, Britannia, also a widow. Her young husband,

The portico overlooks the south lawn and Georgetown Harbor. Legend has it that the three Peter sisters, waving flags from the windows of Tudor Place in Georgetown, and Arlington House and Woodlawn Plantation across the Potomac in Virginia twenty miles away, could see one another.

Commodore Beverley Kennon, killed when a loaded cannon backfired during an exhibition on the USS *Princeton*, left Brittania a single mother at age twenty-nine. She carried on her parents' political activism and commitment to national service. During the Civil War, she and her daughter, Markie Kennon (Martha Custis after her grandmother), made their home into a hostel for Union troops. Markie carried on the family name when she married Armistead Peter, a first cousin, and returned the Peter name to the great house. Their son, Armistead Peter Jr., endowed the Tudor Place Foundation, to which the residence passed after his death in 1984.

And so Tudor Place lives on, virtually unchanged since 1816. The five-and-a-half-acre estate is a rare survivor of the Federal period, as are the gardens, which were laid out at the time the house was built.

Six generations of Peters conducted their affairs from the office in the west wing. The last, Armistead Peter Jr., endowed the Tudor Place Foundation to which the estate passed at his death in 1984. One of the two known letters from General Washington to his wife, Martha, was found hidden in a desk.

KATHARINE GRAHAM HOUSE

1794 | *Architect Unknown*
Enlarged 1878 | *Architect Unknown*

Many antiques and works of art in the drawing room, including the rare eighteenth-century Chinese carpet, came from the Crescent Place house of Mrs. Graham's mother, Agnes E. Meyer.

KATHARINE GRAHAM HAS LIVED IN THE SAME HOUSE FOR MORE THAN HALF A CENTURY. SINCE 1946, IT HAS REMAINED A SINGULAR CONSTANT THROUGH OTHER MAJOR CHANGES IN HER LIFE: HER TWENTY-THREE-YEAR MARRIAGE TO PHILIP L. GRAHAM, PUBLISHER OF THE *WASHINGTON POST*, THEN HIS UNTIMELY DEATH IN 1963, THE REARING OF THEIR FOUR CHILDREN, THE ARRIVAL OF NINE GRANDCHILDREN, AND MRS. GRAHAM'S PERSONAL TRANSFORMATION FROM A SUPPORTIVE SOCIAL DOYENNE TO A LEADING PUBLISHING FORCE IN HER OWN RIGHT, FIRST AS PRESIDENT AND THEN CHAIRMAN OF THE WASHINGTON POST COMPANY. NOW IN HER NINTH DECADE, SHE VIEWS THE THREE-STORY, TWENTY-ROOM RESIDENCE

Works of art in the dining room reflect a lively, eclectic taste, combining Oriental lacquer boxes and screens with Georgian silver and furniture. The bust on the sideboard (above) is of Mrs. Graham's mother.

as a very dear friend. "I still love this house," she says. "It's comfortable, and it works quite well for me alone."

The stately brick house stands secluded in a countrified setting on a major street, among the very few estates developed in antebellum Georgetown's northern woods. The restraint of the cream-painted brick walls and the muted green mansard roof, as well as the set-back against sweeping lawns and the semicircular gravel driveway, create an aura of restraint and guarded security.

The oldest part of the house, encompassing what is now the wide central hall, was built late in the eighteenth century by Thomas Beall, the grandson of Georgetown's single largest original landowner. Even though the house was much smaller than the present structure, the Beall property covered the entire block between Twenty-ninth and Thirtieth, R and Q streets. At the close of the Civil War, the Beall family sold the house and land to Judge Ebenezer Peck of the U.S. Court of Claims. Peck, in turn, sold the western half of the property, where the house stood, to Julia T. Peck. It was under her stewardship that the once modest house acquired its present grandeur, rising to three stories under the mansard roof, with wings to either side of the central entrance.

In 1914, the subsequent owner, Major General William Donovan, retained Washington architect Waddy B. Wood to add the large kitchen wing to the east and remodel the dining room with a neoclassical chair rail, china closets, and a mantel. Then in 1926 Donovan commissioned a grander front door to parallel the house's character, adding the central arched doorway and the raised platform. Symmetry prevails on the classic three-part facade with a large center hall framed by three-story wings, each side reinforced with two bays of full-length windows.

Donovan lived in the house for more than thirty years, throughout his tenure as chief of the Office of Strategic Services and founder of the Central Intelligence Agency. He adored this house as his retreat through the turmoil of World War II, but at war's end, he and twenty-eight-year-old Katharine Graham began negotiating a purchase price. All discussion ended one evening, however, when her father made the deal with the general over dinner. "You did what?" she recalls, in utter disbelief that her father, an astute financier and publisher, agreed to the general's high price.

In 1960, the Grahams undertook an extensive renovation; they gutted the

The oldest part of the house
was built in the late eighteenth
century by Thomas Beale.
The third story and the wings
flanking the central block were
added after the Civil War and
the kitchen wing in 1914.

interior and removed the back porch to extend the house to the fieldstone terrace, the lawn, and the pool, with access through French doors in the rear hall, dining room, and library. They moved out during construction but returned in time to host the inauguration eve party for John F. Kennedy.

In the early 1970s, Mrs. Graham remodeled the principal ground-floor rooms, incorporating her parents' possessions from their Crescent Place house. She refreshed this basic design during the 1980s and again in the early 1990s. A mix of period styles and aesthetic impulses now easily coexist: modern art hangs in the library, eighteenth-century Chinese porcelain, textiles, and paintings grace the dining and living rooms, and French and Georgian chairs, tables, and sofas can be found throughout the house.

The deep rose-red living room mixes eighteenth-century European pieces with rare Oriental treasures Mrs. Graham inherited from her mother. The architecture of the room remains classic, with traditional floor, ceiling, and window moldings set against the ornate white marble mantelpiece, the projecting bay window at one end, and full-length French windows looking out to the long front lawn. With a Renoir painting on one wall and Albrecht Dürer engravings on another, the formality of the setting belies the comfort of this room, the laying-out room, as Mrs. Graham remembers her father calling the living room. Now, it is mostly the room in which she and friends meet weekly for an intense game of contract bridge.

Across the long and spacious entrance hall, the formal dining room extends from the front to the back of the house. It was not always designed this way; in fact, at first it was two rooms: a small formal dining room and a larger "children's" dining room, where most meals were taken. In the early 1970s, once the children had grown and she inherited her parents' Oriental and European antiques, Mrs. Graham opened the two spaces into one.

Taking stock of the Graham house, friend and noted journalist Joseph Alsop chided her, "Darling, when you have a house your size, you must have one big room." She agreed. Moreover, her own life had changed immeasurably. In 1946, her husband of seven years, Philip Graham, succeeded her father as publisher of the *Washington Post*. In 1963, after Philip's death, Katharine became the newspaper's publisher. Rather than hosting receptions and dinners because of her husband's position, she now entertained on the strength of her own stature, often seating over one hundred guests in the enlarged dining room.

The rear of the house opens to the outdoors, the terrace, backyard, and heated pool where she exercises year round. The blanket of green grass is also a private outdoor room for summer dinners, indeed, where Katharine Graham hosted her own eightieth birthday party for 140 well-wishers. The symmetry between Katharine Graham's personal emergence and that of her longtime residence is undeniable: throughout the years, each has graciously evolved.

Adams & Haskins. Archts.
Washington March 23 1854.

1850–1890
THE ROMANTICS

OATSIE CHARLES HOUSE

1854 | *Adams & Haskins*

Built for engraver William H. Dougall in 1854, the house was originally designed in the Italianate villa style in vogue in the mid-nineteenth century. The third story and mansard roof were added in 1875.

MARION SAFFOLD OATS LEITER CHARLES, AN ALABAMA-BORN WASHINGTONIAN, TREASURES HER ROOTS: HER FAMILY HOME IN MONTGOMERY, HER FRIENDS, AND THE DISTINCTION OF THE PLACES SHE HAS LIVED. THESE VALUES STEM FROM HER LIFE IN MONTGOMERY, THE BEAUTIFUL, BUCOLIC TOWN WHERE SHE GREW UP THE GRANDDAUGHTER OF GOVERNOR OATS. "LIFE WAS EXTREMELY INTERESTING AND VERY PLEASANT," SHE REMEMBERS. AS A YOUNG WOMAN, SHE MADE THE GRAND TOUR OF EUROPE EACH SUMMER, DEEPENING WITH EACH TRIP HER KNOWLEDGE AND RESPECT FOR HER OWN COUNTRY'S ARCHITECTURAL HERITAGE.

"I AM VERY, VERY CONSCIOUS OF MY SURROUNDINGS,"

The refined Italianate design of the mid-1800s respected the angularity of neoclassical details, seen in the cornice, window moldings, and double-doorway surround of the living room. Architect George Howell completed the 1960 renovation; Sister Parish and Albert Hadley redesigned the interiors; and designer Anthony Browne has guided the choice of colors, fabrics, and wallpapers.

Oatsie Charles says today. "My house is me." Indeed, the grand old Victorian pile is singularly identified with this sanguine woman, who virtually rescued it from dire straits when she bought it from Ruby Acree in 1959. The walls were stuffed with cotton to keep out the cold, the house a virtual tinder box. Standing on one of the loveliest streets in Georgetown, a mix of brick, stone, stucco, and clapboard historic houses, the Charles residence sits discreetly back from the rumbling traffic of the city.

"Everybody said I was a fool to buy it," she remembers. "But this house looked so charming and romantic sitting here upon the hill." And she, recently widowed, had to have it. Like the 150-year-old American elm tree sweeping its great branch across the front yard, Oatsie Charles is as much a signature of this house as is the mansard roof and Gothic trim. "I have always said that when that old tree dies, I will leave this house."

Engraver and artist William H. Dougall built the two-story house in 1854, when Georgetown was settled with just a few large estates—the Peter family's Tudor Place, Evermay, Dumbarton Oaks, General Grant's house across the street, and the mansion that Katharine Graham now occupies. Sited high above Wisconsin Avenue, the estate enjoyed a countrified setting, surrounded by thick stands of woods and grazing pastures. The house looked very different a hundred years ago. Originally, it was topped by a low-hipped roof and was sparingly styled in the refined Italianate villa fashion popular among affluent homebuilders in the mid-1800s. Similar to the earlier Georgian manner of Tudor Place, Italianate design at mid-century respected the angularity of neoclassical traditions while dressing up exterior and interior faces with ornamental trim—wide bracketed eaves, arched windows framed with heavy molding, a hooded entrance porch, and such decorative niceties as window and roof balconies, tall chimney stacks, and multi-sided bay windows. The main entrance, oriented off-center, suggests the asymmetry of the house's interior floor plan—rooms on the two main floors are arranged irrespective of strict alignments.

William Dougall's house was designed by local architects Adams & Haskins in 1854, just a year after the completion of the Robert P. Dodge house nearby on Twentieth and P streets, designed by Andrew Jackson Downing and his partner Calvert Vaux, America's master architects of the Italianate villa. The Dodge house, with its asymmetrical massing, round-arched windows and doors, prominent porch tower, and airy verandah, no doubt established the local standards for Italianate pattern-book design. The Dougalls' handsome villa followed. Its mansard roof and third story were added in 1875 by the Peck family.

For a year, Oatsie Leiter (in 1969 she married Robert H. Charles, formerly assistant secretary of the Air Force) renovated and restored the house, assisted by architect George Howell, who had earlier restored her Federal-style residence on Q Street when she and Mr. Leiter arrived in Washington in 1942. The library, Mrs. Charles's favorite room, was styled after the Gothic library she had so loved at Strawberry Hill. Aside from this one period-style room, Mrs. Charles says she is "not passionate about the Victorian interior." But she is passionate about her beloved Venetian palace, as she describes it. With its grand living room, intimate dining room, and spacious back-yard and terrace, her house is ideally designed for entertaining friends, diplomats, and cabinet-level appointees. But it is equally comfortable for living, as evidenced by Mrs. Charles's library and her upstairs study. In recent years, Sister Parish and Albert Hadley redesigned the house's interiors, while Mrs. Charles's good friend Anthony Browne has offered guidance on colors, fabrics, and wallpaper schemes.

Whether in Montgomery, Washington, or Newport, Rhode Island (where she and her husband have a summer home), Mrs. Charles has always lived amid tradition in a historic residence. She asks a thoughtful question, one that implies a wise and intuitive understanding of architectural scale and the nature of buildings: "What do you think of the state of restoration in America today?" Pausing, she answers her own question. "Fewer and fewer people care about beauty today," Mrs. Charles laments. Now in her late seventies, she spends her days in the avocation of preservation and philanthropy. In Newport, she chairs the Newport Restoration Foundation and the Doris Duke Foundation, a commitment both to her late friend and to her own values about roots and place.

A rich profusion of detail pervades every room. In Mrs. Charles's second-floor bedroom, the fur bedspread and linen shams complement the black walnut four-poster bed and gilt mirrors. This room, high above the city's treetops, looks out to the spires of National Cathedral and Rock Creek Park.

KITTY KELLEY HOUSE

1840s | *Architect Unknown*

The Kelley house sits in seclusion atop a wooded hill, thus affording a great deal of privacy. Here, Kelley wrote several of her infamous celebrity biographies, including those of Frank Sinatra and Nancy Reagan.

PERHAPS IT IS THE NANCY AND RONNIE REAGAN CALLING-CARD HOLDER ON THE KITCHEN COUNTER OR THE COLLECTION OF PUNDIT CARTOONS ABOUT KITTY KELLEY AND HER BOOK SUBJECTS THAT COVERS THE WALLS OF THE POWDER ROOM THAT REVEAL THE IDENTITY OF THIS HISTORIC RESIDENCE'S OWNER. INDEED, FOR ALL THE CLUES, THE GOTHIC BRICK COTTAGE IS PROBABLY UNEXPECTED AS THE HOME OF BIOGRAPHER KITTY KELLEY. BUT SHE HAS LIVED AND WORKED HERE FOR TWENTY YEARS, AND SINCE 1992, SHE HAS SHARED THE RESIDENCE WITH HER SECOND HUSBAND, ALLERGIST JOHN ZUCKER.

SET HIGH ABOVE A DENSELY SHADED STREET IN GEORGETOWN, THE HOUSE IS VIRTUALLY

invisible from the sidewalk. Built in the late 1840s or early 1850s, it adjoins a large frame house, which was built around 1800. The smaller house was originally designed in a simplified version of the Italianate style popular in the 1840s, without the wooden carpentry on the gables, and might have been built as an addition for younger or extended family members, a practice common in the nineteenth century.

During the economic prosperity of the post–Civil War years, the owners adorned both houses with gingerbread carpentry. Also during this period, Mayor Alexander "Boss" Shepherd undertook his public improvement campaign, and the original street was leveled by a deep cut, leaving the property sitting on a high bank of earth. Throughout the nineteenth and into the twentieth century, the adjoining houses were well cared for by successive owners. In 1945, they were acquired by a news commentator who rented the brick cottage to Justice William Brennan in 1956, the same year he was appointed to the Supreme Court. The justice, who wrote over thirteen hundred opinions—most notably Roe v. Wade (1973)—and most of the groundbreaking preservation laws, such as Penn Central v. New York City (1978), lived in this charming historic house for twenty-two years.

Supreme Court Justice William Brennan, who lived in the house for twenty-two years, wrote many important opinions, including Roe v. Wade, sitting at a card table in the living room.

Kitty Kelley, a biographer who prizes her reputation as a candid chronicler of the private lives of such icons as Frank Sinatra, Nancy Reagan, and Britain's royal family, actually depends on the quietude of this hilltop site, secluded in the center of town at the edge of a steep rock terrace. In fact, she has seen no other house she likes as much and finds herself unable to leave. "I've tried to move," she explains, "but this house has a hold on me."

The success of her 1991 biography of Nancy Reagan enabled Kelley to renovate and redecorate the entire house. The mandarin-red living room and the book-lined oak library were organized with the professional assistance of Ken Jennings Design of New York, but the deep sapphire-blue dining room is Kelley's own creation, executed in a period-style Victorian motif, as is the upstairs master bedroom suite.

The grounds surrounding her house where she has hosted innumerable fund-raisers, memorials, showers, birthdays, Christmas Day open houses, and weddings (even her own wedding to John, with three hundred guests in attendance), commands just as much of her attention as the interiors. A topiary deer and dancing bear stand watch over the entrance; nearby, topiary monkeys hang from a magnolia tree. The flower garden that borders the brick patio near the smokehouse "blooms with so many flowers," Kitty explains, because her beloved cats "are all buried back there." Runt, however, a descendant of Ernest Hemingway's Key West cats, is alive and well and enjoys the run of house and garden.

"It must have been a wonderful neighborhood," she muses, thinking back to the time in the 1960s when Justice Brennan lived in her house, writing at his card table in what is now her living room, and Justice Frankfurter lived across the street. "It makes me feel safe living here," she says, "because of whose home it was before."

Although Kelley worked with a New York decorator for much of the house, the dining room is her own design. She and her husband entertain frequently, having begun with their own garden wedding and reception in 1992.

SUSAN MARY ALSOP HOUSE

1885–87 | *Architect Unknown*

*The drawing room is
one of the most elegant
in Washington, with French
doors extending the room
to the garden.*

FOR SUSAN MARY JAY PATTEN ALSOP, EACH OF
HER HOMES HAS MARKED A MEMORABLE TIME IN
HER EXTRAORDINARY LIFE. NOW, THE SOCIAL
DOYENNE OF OLD GEORGETOWN IS CONTENT TO
LIVE QUIETLY IN THE COMFORT OF HER LATE
MOTHER'S HISTORIC BRICK TOWN HOUSE, WHICH
SHE INHERITED IN 1978. THE HOUSE HAS BEEN IN
THE JAY FAMILY SINCE HER MOTHER ACQUIRED IT
IN 1943. HERE, MRS. ALSOP HAS BROUGHT
TOGETHER THE HEIRLOOMS AND PERSONAL TREA-
SURES ACCUMULATED BY FIVE GENERATIONS
OF AN AMERICAN DIPLOMATIC FAMILY. ALL
THROUGH THE HOUSE, FAMILY FURNITURE FILLS
THE ROOMS AND PHOTOGRAPHS OF HER CHIL-
DREN AND GRANDCHILDREN LINE THE HALLWAYS.

Rooms of deep forest green and crimson, sky blue and soft apricot, contain an eclectic mix of eighteenth-century French and Italian antiques and twentieth-century American and English portraits.

Mrs. Alsop appears every bit the gentle Washington patrician, a woman who has seen much and been seen by many presidents, ambassadors, foreign-service officers, and journalists from around the globe. Her 1880s town house represents a graceful time warp back to the turn of the century.

Born in Rome in 1918, the daughter of diplomats and a descendant of first Supreme Court Chief Justice John Jay, a teenage Susan Mary Jay first arrived in Washington, D.C., after her father's foreign tour had ended. She met William Patten, a State Department officer in New York, and they married in 1939 and returned in 1941 to wartime Washington. Patten was a friend of Franklin Roosevelt, Jr., and he and his wife soon became occasional dinner guests at the White House.

As World War II drew to a close, the American embassy in Paris beckoned Bill Patten. Residing there throughout the 1950s was a welcome change for Susan Mary, who had diplomatic service in her blood and hosted

The drawing room is filled with eighteenth-century French and Italian heirlooms of Mrs. Alsop's diplomatic family, which includes John Jay, a signer of the Declaration of Independence and the first Chief Justice of the Supreme Court. The framed photograph on the desk is of the columnist/ journalist Joseph Alsop, her late former husband.

Known as the "little red sitting room," this drawing room is Mrs. Alsop's favorite. Above the mantel hangs a portrait of her father, Peter A. Jay, painted by John Singer Sargent in 1890.

such luminaries as Winston Churchill, Evelyn Waugh, and Charles de Gaulle.

In 1960, after her husband died, Susan Mary Patten returned to Washington to begin a new phase of life as a single mother of two young children. Within the year she married Washington insider and journalist Joseph Alsop. For them, as for all Democrats in Washington, these were exciting times. John F. Kennedy had won the election and brought with him a fresh generation of young diplomats and economists. A new crowd was buying up Georgetown houses, gentrifying the working-class neighborhood, and the Alsops' home became a focal point of social and political activity, a place where journalists and politicians dined often and stayed late—most notably President Kennedy on the eve of the Cuban missile crisis.

After thirteen years of marriage, the Alsops divorced. She settled into her late mother's house, a private place shrouded by leafy trees along the street and a mature garden out back. Mrs. Alsop began to write again—publishing a biography of Lady Sackville and *Yankees at the Court*—and to renovate her historic home, creating brilliant French settings to "de-pompify" her mother's musty silk damask interior.

The garden room seats eighteen and "is extremely good for entertaining," Mrs. Alsop says. The drawing room, "the little red room," as she calls it, is her favorite, "a very personal room and one I use a great, great deal." She designed this room around John Singer Sargent's portrait of her father as a child, choosing the wallpaper and chintz to complement its red velvet frame. It also houses her collection of French porcelain monkeys, acquired during the years she and Bill Patten were stationed in Paris. The blue dining room, which has hosted First Lady Nancy Reagan (to introduce California's first lady to Georgetown society) and Pamela Harriman, is plainer than other such dining rooms, though still formal, letting people dominate the decor.

Mrs. Alsop's well-worn second-floor study is obviously the room of a writer. Walls are lined floor to ceiling with books, and an old American desk that has traveled to Paris and back is tucked in the corner. The room centers around a small sofa and a card table piled high with papers, where she usually writes, reads, or simply relaxes.

These days, Susan Mary Jay Patten Alsop begins each morning with a walk through Georgetown, taking in Dumbarton Oaks or Montrose Park, or passing by the nearby estates of good friends Katharine Graham or Oatsie Charles. The image of understated elegance, she is a fixture on the neighborhood's brick sidewalks, walking steadily as she leans lightly on her cane. While life in Georgetown has become less peaceful and more commercial than in decades past, Mrs. Alsop maintains that it is "the most agreeable, most cheerful, lovely place in Washington."

A contributing editor of Architectural Digest *and author of several books including* Yankees at the Court, *Mrs. Alsop uses this room for reading and working.*

George S. Fraser House
1890 | *Hornblower & Marshall*

Joseph Hornblower House
1897 | *Hornblower & Marshall*

Joseph Hornblower designed the Fraser house and his own residence in an Italian Renaissance style that incorporates Romanesque influences. Both houses were of clean line, natural materials, and intricate brick work with limestone detailing, as seen in the entrance hall of the Fraser house (opposite). Today Jay Pagano (above) owns the Hornblower house; the Fraser house is the headquarters of the Church of Scientology.

Some critics have described architect Joseph Hornblower as a social climber. A preacher's son who majored in philosophy at Yale University, Hornblower went abroad to apprentice in the Paris atelier of Jean-Louis Pascal. Upon settling in Washington, he placed himself squarely in the company of his clientele and vigorously pursued memberships in Washington's Cosmos, Metropolitan, and Chevy Chase clubs, as well as New York City's Century, University, and National Arts clubs. His business partner, James Marshall, also lunched at the same clubs and attended the black-tie balls of Washington society.

Built for a wealthy capitalist in 1890, the Fraser house on Dupont Circle had become a restaurant by the 1950s. In the 1990s, the Church of Scientology restored the mansion, giving its new church a residential feeling. The dining room became a chapel (right), and the original library is the office of L. Ron Hubbard, founder of the Church of Scientology. The tooled leather wall panels and the oak stairhall (opposite) were restored to their original condition.

The two young architects, roommates and former colleagues in the Treasury's supervising architect's office, established the firm of Hornblower & Marshall in 1883. Hornblower was the marketeer and architectural stylist of the firm, and Marshall the interior designer known for his exquisite use of textiles. During the 1890s, Hornblower & Marshall rose to become Washington's top residential designers. Their style drew from popular Romanesque and neoclassical genres and emphasized clean lines and flat surfaces with only minimal ornament. The use of natural materials, a design principle popularized in stick and shingle style designs after the 1870s, became a trademark of Hornblower & Marshall's work, in masonries of deep red, yellow, and brown brick and limestone.

When New York capitalist George S. Fraser moved to Washington in 1890, he retained Hornblower & Marshall—and paid almost $80,000—to build his Italian Renaissance–style residence on Dupont Circle, a few blocks north of the elegant mansions on Massachusetts Avenue. Looking out to Connecticut Avenue, this brilliant red brick and limestone structure remains among the best known of Hornblower & Marshall's buildings. The layout and decorative detailing of the main-floor rooms are typical of the period—the great hall at center (a dark, oak-paneled room with a cherubic fireplace of carved

In the 1980s Jay Pagano converted the Hornblower house
into four spacious apartments,
retaining the first and second
for his own use. Pagano's
drawing room (opposite)
reflects the character of the
original residence. A stairway
is concealed behind the
fireplace and large French
doors open to a south-
facing garden.

limestone) surrounded by the paneled dining room, formal living room, the sitting room with beam-and-leather ceiling, and private library. History has
recorded little about George Fraser, other than that he built this residence and
died ten years later. His widow sold the house in 1901 to Miriam Thropp,
daughter of Abraham Lincoln's assistant secretary of war during the Civil War.
The Thropps entertained lavishly, even while retail shops and eateries moved
in around them to preside over the former residential neighborhood.

Commerce arrived on the Thropps' front portico by the 1930s. For almost
five decades, high-end restaurants occupied this former residence, attracted to
the choice Dupont Circle business location. By 1990, however, the century-old
house beckoned for an owner of means, a steward to repair the structure and
update building systems, and to restore Hornblower & Marshall's intricate
interior of oak, plaster, leather, and limestone.

It was the Church of Scientology, in search of a Washington home for
L. Ron Hubbard's Founding Church, that acquired the landmark residence in
1994. The Scientologists made significant character changes in particular
rooms to convert the house-turned-restaurant into a church. On the main level,
the original living room, the largest and most formal, became a counseling area
for new members and a bookstore for Hubbard's prolific writings. The dining
room was turned into a chapel for religious services, and capitalist George
Fraser's intimate oak library was reincarnated as Hubbard's office, furnished
with his books, 1950s desk, and world globe that he had when he founded the
Church of Scientology. Fraser's basement wine cellar became the church's
"cleansing room" for new parishioners.

Across Connecticut Avenue on secluded Hillyer Place, a one-block, one-
way street named for Curtis J. Hillyer (one of the land venturers in the California syndicate that laid out the Dupont Circle area and whose estate covered
this property) is the residence of architect Joseph Hornblower. At age fifty,
Hornblower married his first cousin, Caroline French, and designed this large
four-story house for himself and his bride. He built his residence in the Dupont
Circle neighborhood, centered among residences he and Marshall had
designed for Duncan Phillips, Mabel Boardman, Alvin Lothrop, and Mrs.
Alexander Graham Bell. Free to do as he pleased for his own house, Hornblower liberated his eclectic impulses to strip the form down to one clean, rectangular mass, a theme he repeated in recessed windows, paneled woodwork,
and the open floor plans. Whimsy and restraint mix in this 1897 avant-garde
design. Hornblower marked each floor with subtle transitions in the color of
the exterior brick, from dark brown at ground level, to a lighter ochre on the
second and third, to beige on the fourth level, topped by an airy white brick
layer below the restrained Greek cornice.

The Hornblowers had no children, and when Joseph died suddenly in

The Hague just ten years after they wed, Caroline chose to remain in the Dupont Circle house and rent the upper floors to a young couple, Augustas and Flora Downing, who bought the house a decade later. The residence has remained a private home for more than a century. After the Hornblowers and the Downings, Walker Stone, editor of the Scripts Howard News chain, and his wife, Donna, lived here for forty-one years. The house is now occupied by Jay Pagano, who acquired it from the Stone estate in 1984.

When Pagano first moved in, he imagined he had walked onto the stage set of *Great Expectations;* the musty Victorian pile had not seen a paint brush in twenty-five years. The integrity of Hornblower's design, however, remained intact. Pagano, a civil rights lawyer who worked under Associate Justice Clarence Thomas at the Equal Employment Opportunity Commission, knew virtually nothing about Hornblower & Marshall or the provenance of the house he had acquired. He soon became interested as he prepared to renovate with architect Michael Holt, whose first priority was to preserve the house to the greatest extent possible. The open room layouts led Pagano to renovate the residence into four loft apartments, three rentals, and his own residence. "It is fascinating," notes Pagano, "that a Victorian architect, when

WILLIAM & LUCINDA SEALE HOUSE

1895 | *William Jameson*

The house was very up-to-date when it was built by developer William Jameson in 1895. This central living hall was all the rage at that time and is still the place of choice to sit when the Seales entertain.

FEW CAN RIVAL WILLIAM SEALE'S KNOWLEDGE OF AMERICAN HOUSE INTERIORS. YET IN HIS OWN LIFE HE CHOOSES COMFORT OVER HISTORICAL ACCURACY, LIVING IN AN 1895 TOWN HOUSE FILLED WITH AN ASSORTMENT OF INHERITED FURNITURE AND FAMILY TREASURES, AND COLLECTIBLES ACQUIRED FROM TEXAS TO BOSTON. IT SEEMS PERFECT THAT THE WHITE HOUSE HISTORIAN AND AUTHOR OF THE DEFINITIVE TWO-VOLUME HISTORY, *THE PRESIDENT'S HOUSE*, SHOULD LIVE IN THIS NINETEENTH-CENTURY RESIDENCE IN OLD-TOWN ALEXANDRIA.

NATIVE SOUTHERNERS WILLIAM AND LUCINDA SEALE WERE ACTUALLY HEADED FOR NEW YORK WHEN THEY MADE A DETOUR TO ALEXANDRIA,

The upstairs sitting room is
now an office for Lucinda
Seale. The fireplace is draped
in Victorian style and the
wallpaper is by Schumacher.

an unexpected turn in the road that has lasted almost three decades. Initially, the Seales had their eye on this three-story brick Victorian, but it was not for sale. They settled instead for an older house a few blocks down Prince Street. William Seale soon became fast friends with the house's two elderly owners, Corina and Lucie Reardon (the daughters of William Reardon, who had owned the house since 1899). Once the Reardon sisters retired and were ready to move, they telephoned William. The Seales and Reardons had only to settle on a price, a detail barely agreed to when the Seales moved their furniture into the house in December 1974. Here they have raised their family and here they expect to stay as long as they live, in the shadow of the nation's capital.

The intensity of the colors and the furnishings make the front parlor a very Victorian room. Some of the objects, inherited from William Seale's Uncle Oliver, who "in spite of being a Yankee was a good story-teller" give the room more a feeling of period New York or Boston.

After receiving a doctorate in history at Duke University, William Seale first followed the traditional academic route, as an assistant professor at Lamar University in Texas, then the University of South Carolina at Columbia. But his love of old houses and the stories they tell kept speaking to him. He decided to leave academia for a life in restoration, and since the early 1970s, he has conducted scores of restoration projects and has written fifteen books.

While his own house may not possess the same historicism as the houses he gets paid to restore, in the town of Alexandria this Roman brick house represented the cutting edge of residential design and domestic technology when local developer William Jameson completed it in 1895. No doubt Jameson meant to exhibit his talents as a contractor as much as he intended to advertise his good financial standing. The developer profited handsomely as post–Civil War Alexandria developed into a railway nexus during Virginia's reconstruction-era boom, a solid departure for the eighteenth-century tobacco and grain seaport. Jameson's own house stood on fashionable Prince Street among other new residences going up, away from the congested riverfront district across South Washington Street. Alexandria's narrow grid streets have sprouted a virtual museum of eighteenth- and nineteenth-century brick and frame town houses, most semi-detached and attached rowhouses. Amid the pleasant scale of this dense environment, freestanding residences surrounded by yards and sculptured gardens command notice. In this way, the Seales' house suggests a certain level of quality in the spacious floor plan, the central living hall (all the rage in 1895), the sensible flow of first-floor rooms, the five second-floor bedrooms including the master bedroom with a private fireplace and live-in maid's quarters on the third floor with a back stairway leading directly to the kitchen. Central heating and up-to-the-moment plumbing in the bathrooms, oak woodwork on the first floor and cheaper pine in the private second and third floors all indicate an ambitious building program executed on a limited budget.

The Seales describe themselves as "house people." As they both work at home, each day they occupy all three floors. William's office and mammoth book collection (some 4,500 volumes) take up most of the third floor. Lucinda, who is active nationally in competitive flower arranging, has her studio-office in the front room of the second floor. She also has taken the Reardon sisters' "funny idea of a garden," as William describes it, and redesigned and nursed it into a spacious garden that peaks in late spring. While the Seales seem a bit self-conscious about decorating their own house "not so correctly," a 1906 walnut dining room table from the Seale family farm in Texas, and the Lincoln-era mementos from an uncle who was a wonderful story-teller even if he was a Yankee, and "this and that" from Lucinda's family in The Plains, Virginia, their home, as it should, tells a full story about the Seales and their extended family from generations past.

Many of the objects in the house come from Lucinda Seale's old family home, The Plains, near Manassas, Virginia.

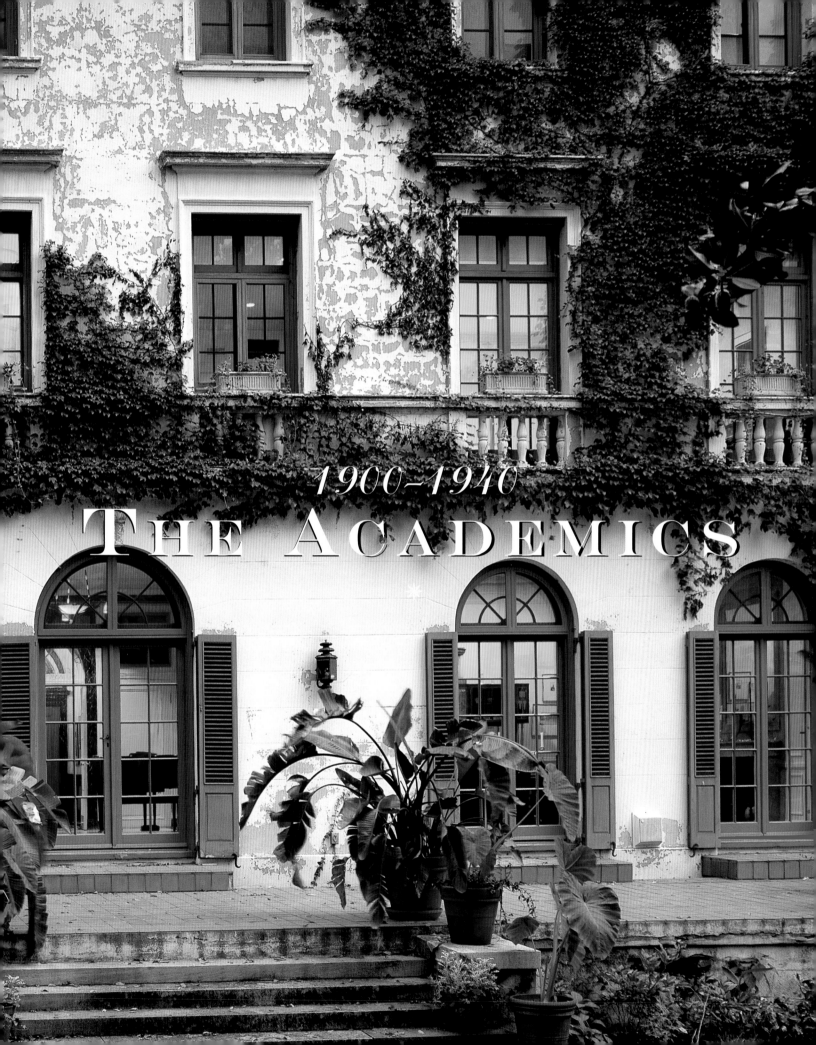

1900–1940
The Academics

LARZ & ISABEL ANDERSON HOUSE

1902–05 | *Little & Browne*

Designed by Boston architects Little & Browne, Anderson Houses was destined to become the headquarters of the Society of the Cincinnati. The two-story marble music room (above) is the house's masterpiece, with a flying staircase for guests to look down from the balcony to the scene below. A sun-filled arcade of paned windows along the rear facade opens out to the garden and connects the morning room (opposite), conservatory, and Isabel's sitting room.

LARZ AND ISABEL WELD PERKINS ANDERSON, WHO BUILT THE ANDERSON HOUSE, WERE BOTH BORN INTO MASSACHUSETTS FAMILIES WITH A TRADITION OF ARCHITECTURAL PATRONAGE. LARZ'S FAMILY ARRIVED IN THE NATION'S CAPITAL IN 1884, AT THE DAWN OF THE GILDED AGE OF ART AND POLITICS. HIS FATHER, NICHOLAS L. ANDERSON, A CIVIL WAR GENERAL AND BOSTON BRAHMIN, COMMISSIONED HIS HARVARD CLASS-MATE HENRY HOBSON RICHARDSON TO BUILD HIS FAMILY'S FIRST HOUSE IN WASHINGTON NEAR THE DOUBLE HOUSE HE HAD DESIGNED FOR TWO OTHER CLASSMATES, HENRY ADAMS AND JOHN HAY. THE ANDERSONS' SANDSTONE HOUSE WAS LOCATED AT THE SOUTHWEST CORNER OF

Fifteenth and K streets; the Hay-Adams double house stood on the northwest corner of Lafayette Square (both have been demolished).

Nicholas and Elizabeth Anderson frequently wrote to their son Larz, a student at Harvard, about the notoriety of their residence as it emerged from ground level, and about the pleasure of working with Richardson. After a year-long tour of Europe Larz attended Harvard Law School and then returned to Washington to establish his own household and began a diplomatic career. In 1897 he married Isabel Perkins, heiress to her grandfather's East Indian trading fortune, who became an author whose books combined her love of both children and literature in delightful tales of nymphs, gods, and goddesses. As the son of a Civil War general and descendant of a Revolutionary War officer, Larz valued civic duty to one's country and city. Family connections dominated in the mosaic of his life, and it was at the recommendation of John Hay, a confidante of his grandfather, that he accepted a diplomatic post under Robert Todd Lincoln, ambassador to the Court of St. James, and began a career in foreign service in which he rose to become the minister to Belgium and ambassador to Japan.

The Andersons began planning their Washington house soon after they married in 1902, selecting a site west of Dupont Circle on Massachusetts Avenue, an address then emerging as one of the best in town. The Andersons chose two young Boston architects who had worked in Richardson's office, Arthur Little and Herbert W. C. Browne. (Little & Browne also designed the Andersons' country house, Weld, in Brookline, Massachusetts.) Once completed in 1905, the Andersons' limestone residence, among the largest and most expensive of its day in Washington, soon became known for lavish entertaining. The perfectly symmetrical design—styled after English baroque architecture—distinguished itself on the grandiose avenue by the massive pedimented gates across the front, flanked by wings and a circular portico set back against the sweeping drive. An eclectic mix of French and English Beaux-Arts traditions adorned the interior.

The masterpiece was the two-story, marble music room, for which Larz asked Little and Browne to include a flying staircase so that guests might ascend to a balcony and look down upon the scene below.

The great hall connects the public hall and drawing, dining, and smoking rooms. "Its approaches and succession of rooms," Larz Anderson wrote in his diary, make it a suitable background for dignitaries and foreign guests.

The windowless stone front has sometimes been regarded as forbidding and unwelcoming, yet the great arched gates might also be seen as passages from the public street into the private domain, tying the house to the street and the city around it. At the back of the house, the sun-filled arcade of paned windows opens out to the garden and connects the morning room, conservatory, and Isabel's sitting room, all private spaces where the Andersons spent a good deal of time. The architects assiduously segregated public rooms (the great hall, music room, dining room, and salon) from private spaces (the library, morning room, Larz's cypress den, and Isabel's sitting room). Family bedrooms and private sitting rooms occupied the second floor, with sixteen bedrooms for dignitaries and six servants' rooms above.

Clearly this residence was designed to be more than a family home. "It was arranged for stately functions of a limited size," Larz wrote in his day book, "and its approaches and succession of rooms make a suitable background" for dignitaries and foreign guests. The King and Queen of Siam (now Thailand) stayed here during their state visit in 1931, while Larz and Isabel were on holiday in Gibraltar. The royal aides occupied Larz's den, while American military and naval aides took over the library; the secret service closeted itself in the housekeeper's office. "The entourage just filled the house comfortably," Larz concluded.

The Andersons had a genuine interest in building a residence that contributed to Washington's design by "directing its development along the lines of beauty prepared for it," Larz wrote in 1929. Inspired by his great-grandfather Nicholas Longworth, a founder of the Society of the Cincinnati (the patriotic society founded in 1783 for descendants of Army and Navy officers in the Revolutionary War) with George Washington, Larz Anderson intended that the residence's lasting legacy was to serve as the national home of the society. The American eagle, the Society's emblem, dominates the building's public passages: it appears sculpted into the pediment over the main portico entrance, in the fresco of the great hall, and on the ceiling of the salon. In commemoration of the Society's tenets, marble and mahogany-paneled walls throughout the house are adorned with Anderson family artifacts—a bust of its founder, Nicholas Longworth, a mural of great-uncle Major Robert Anderson at Fort Sumter, Belgian tapestries from the Andersons' diplomatic tours, gifts from Louis XIII to Cardinal Barberini, and formal portraits of Isabel and Larz dressed in the full regalia of national medals and honorary ribbons. The room at the top of the great staircase showcases scenic wall paintings by Mowbray commemorating the Society.

The Andersons lent permanence in Washington's transient diplomatic corps and political *cum* social set, from one administration to another. They frequently dined at the White House and foreign embassies, and little escaped Larz's social calendar and Isabel's good works, mostly for the American Red Cross. They counted the Charles Francis Adamses, the William Howard Tafts, and the Richard Townsends among their longest and dearest friends. Larz and Isabel respected the old order's ritualistic conventions, even against the mounting pressures of twentieth-century progress. "We remained the only house in Washington, except the Embassies, which turned out the servants in full-dress livery, shorts and stockings, buckled shoes and braided coast," Larz admitted in 1929. Yet, in a bittersweet way, they also knew that such customs were dated. Even while these loyal Democrats were happy for the presence of the Roosevelt administration in town, throughout the 1930s they saw their beloved city "going to pot, streets filthy, police inefficient, Congress running wild." Perhaps the passing of the old guard was not so easy after all.

For all the pomp and circumstance in their lives, Larz and Isabel Anderson lived comfortably and informally in their Massachusetts Avenue mansion. They treasured their life together, and especially their quiet evenings in Larz's den. After his death in 1937, Isabel published her husband's journals, as well as her own children's stories. Anderson House passed to the Society of the Cincinnati in 1938 and is now open to the public as a house museum.

JIM & KATE LEHRER HOUSE

1906 | *Arthur B. Heaton, Architect*

The Lehrers chose this Cleveland Park house in 1979 because it was perfect for their family's cherished possessions (thousands of books, Jim's rare collection of bus signs and miniature buses, and Kate's Victorian furniture from her Kentucky childhood and a convenient drive to the PBS station in Arlington, where Jim puts together the "Lehrer News Hour."

EVEN AS JIM LEHRER LEAVES HIS CLEVELAND PARK HOUSE EACH MORNING FOR A LONG DAY OF PUTTING TOGETHER THE "LEHRER NEWS HOUR" ON PBS, AND HIS WIFE, KATE LEHRER, SPENDS HER DAYS IMPECCABLY RESEARCHING AND WRITING BEST-SELLING HISTORICAL NOVELS, THEY MAINTAIN AN UNASSUMING LIFE AT HOME.

THEY AND THEIR THREE DAUGHTERS, JAMIE, LUCY, AND AMANDA, ARRIVED IN WASHINGTON FROM TEXAS IN THE EARLY 1970S, AND MOVED INTO THE DISTRICT (WHERE THEY HAD ALWAYS WANTED TO BE) IN 1979. THE SON OF A BUS DRIVER, JIM GREW UP IN TEXAS, IN THE PANHANDLE TOWN OF VICTORIA, AND KATE, WHILE BORN IN TEXAS, GREW UP IN KENTUCKY. THEIR NATIVE ROOTS

are deeply embedded in their lives, and are reflected throughout their home. Indeed, their lives are mirrored in the rooms and family possessions of this turn-of-the-century house, a large pebble-stuccoed residence located high on a hill overlooking the city and the National Cathedral. The dining room's Eastlake-style Victorian furnishings reflect Kate's Kentucky heritage; Jim's "bus room" in the basement, which houses his collection of miniature buses, reveals his intimate connection with his father as well as his own days working as a Trailways ticket agent while attending Victoria College. Old English influences, such as the mighty brick chimney, small-paned windows, shingled gambrel roof, and sprawling wings to the side and rear, complete the eclectic mix of styles.

The thousands of books packed tightly into the large, oak-lined library—and every inch of the house, including stairways, chairs, under beds, and on tables—reveal each family member's deep respect

Jim Lehrer's "bus room" is his basement retreat, the place where he goes to write and to remember his Texas boyhood. Thousands of books are packed into to oak-paneled library (opposite), and throughout the house, revealing the Lehrers' love of words and literature.

for words, literature, and publishing. Jamie, the Lehrers' eldest daughter, writes children's books, and Lucy, a playright, won the Helen Hayes Award, Jim's tenth novel, *White Widow*, the story of a middle-aged bus driver in Texas in the 1950s, is based on his own and his father's experiences. Kate's third novel, *Out of Eden*, which won the Western Heritage Award for fiction and was adapted for television, tells the tale of two well-born women who leave Paris to homestead in Kansas in the early 1900s.

The house was commissioned in 1906 by Charles and Esther Neill. The Neills chose Arthur Heaton, a popular Washington residential architect who had designed a handful of houses in the Cleveland Park district, to design their residence. The house, an elegant arts-and-crafts rendition with an abundance of wings, dormers, and porches, must have stood as one of the finest of its day. Heaton, a native Washingtonian, knew his craft as well as any residential architect working locally: he apprenticed with local architects, studied for a year at the Sorbonne in Paris, and returned home to design over a thousand projects for such major land developers as Shannon & Luchs

Kate Lehrer has made the second-floor sleeping porch into her study. Windows wrap the house on all sides, filling rooms with light.

and the Chevy Chase Land Company, which created Cleveland Park.

Within a decade after the house was completed, the Neills acquired the adjacent lot to the west, where they built a two-story wing with a windowed sleeping porch on the second floor, which is now Kate's study. The library wing, opening out from this addition and the rear sun porch, appears to have been added later, in the 1920s or 1930s. Concealed behind a high hedge, this house serves as a refuge of sorts for the Lehrers. "My energy just diffuses when I walk in," Kate explains. "It's a place of real tranquility."

This house has been owned and occupied by only four families in its eight decades, one of these for a brief three years. The Neills lived out their lives here. In 1953, *New Republic* publisher Gilbert Harrison and his wife, Anne, bought the house. They, like the Lehrers, wrote books. When the Lehrers were looking for a house to buy in the late 1970s, they searched for a home with two writing rooms, five bedrooms, and plenty of space for books. They knew this house was their home the first time they saw it.

Kate Lehrer's comfortable touch is everywhere. In collaboration with her friend and designer Saski Weinstein of New York, she designed each room with light and multiple colors. Having lived most of her life in the south, she needs sunshine, lots of it. Groups of windows wrap this house on all sides, filling rooms with abundant sunlight.

Most people are familiar with the image of Jim Lehrer the newsman and commentator in control of the camera. Kate Lehrer is regarded as one of Washington's premier hostesses, even though, she says, they don't entertain much except for book parties for such friends as Howard Adams, Roger Rosenblatt, and Robin MacNeil. In all, the ambiance of normality in this home is unexpected, and is made even more striking by Jim's bus room, Kate's comfortable clutter (mostly books and magazines) all around, and their all-American 1940s-style kitchen. While Jim Lehrer required more time than his family to feel like he "belonged" to this house, he now says "it's a part of me, I feel that it's mine, it is spiritually very familiar."

New York designer Saski Weinstein has helped the Lehrers to create a comfortable rooms filled with antique furnishings, Jim's minature buses, and cherished mementos of their three daughters.

The dining room in George Eatman's apartment at the Dresden combines furnishings from various eighteenth- and nineteenth-century styles. Above the sideboard is a portrait of his grandmother and her two daughters painted in 1916.

THE DRESDEN

1909–10 | *Albert H. Beers, Architect*
| *Harry Wardman, Developer*

The GENTLE BOW OF THE DRESDEN ECHOES THE SWEEP OF CONNECTICUT AVENUE AS IT RISES FROM DUPONT CIRCLE AND CONTINUES ACROSS ROCK CREEK BRIDGE TOWARD CLEVELAND PARK. TWO DECADES BEFORE DEVELOPER HARRY WARDMAN BUILT THE DRESDEN, THE AREA WAS THICKLY WOODED AND BEYOND OFFICIAL DISTRICT BOUNDARIES. THE CHEVY CHASE LAND COMPANY CHANGED ALL THAT WHEN SENATOR FRANCIS NEWLANDS OF NEVADA (THE STATE THAT WAS THE SPECULATIVE CAPITAL OF NORTH AMERICA) BACKED THE PROPERTY INVESTORS IN A MASSIVE TRACT PURCHASE ENCOMPASSING CONNECTICUT AVENUE AND ROCK CREEK PARK, THEN SUPPORTED FEDERAL HIGHWAY LEGISLATION

The graceful curve of the
entrance hall echoes the
rounded form of the Dresden
as it follows the curve of Connecticut Avenue.

to extend roads and city services to the property. The Highway Acts of 1893 and 1898 made the northwest district between Florida and Western avenues part of the city and literally paved the way for the northward expansion of residential neighborhoods and subdivisions.

By the turn of the century, Connecticut Avenue around California Street seemed destined for residential development. In the years following the Civil War, as Congress transformed the federal city from an armed camp to the capital of a unified nation, the city paved the six-block stretch of Connecticut Avenue between the White House and Dupont Circle. The blocks immediately north of the Circle were paved soon after, during Alexander "Boss" Shepherd's public works extravaganza when Congress appointed the speculative developer governor of the District from 1871 to 1874. During the 1880s and 1890s, Connecticut Avenue emerged as downtown's main commercial street, anchored at one end by the White House and Lafayette Square mansions and at the other by Dupont Circle and Massachusetts Avenue mansions. Elite gentleman's clubs, embassies, and consulates lined the surrounding blocks. The Dupont Circle neighborhood rapidly filled with row houses and duplexes, a haven for middle-class professionals. Then as now, it was an urbane neighborhood in the midst of wealthy, architect-designed residential enclaves: Sixteenth Street's Meridian Hill, the tree-shaded Massachusetts Avenue between Thomas and Sheridan circles, and the Kalorama Triangle area west of Connecticut Avenue.

Residential expansion marched north on the rising land along and around Connecticut Avenue. With electric streetcar lines traveling up to Cleveland Park by the turn of the century, luxury apartment builders saw magnificent potential in the undeveloped blocks north of California Street. Developers set off a veritable construction binge of high-rise luxury apartment buildings elegantly fitted out with rooftop terraces, balconies, and sunrooms. Eight luxury buildings, including the Highlands, Westmoreland, Woodward, and Altamont, arose nearby one another around Connecticut Avenue and California Street to Rock Bridge between 1900 and 1920, a remarkable record during an era of no land-use regulations to guide developers in building certain types, sizes, and heights of buildings in specific areas. (Congress passed the first zoning law in 1920.)

Even in this environment, Harry Wardman stood in a class of his own making, a prolific apartment and residential builder in early-twentieth-century Washington. The Dresden was among his best buildings, and one of the finest on the avenue. Certainly he captured one of the prime sites with clear vistas across Rock Creek Bridge and unobstructed views of the park. Wardman's chief architect, Albert H. Beers, created a building that mixed European classicism of the French Beaux-Arts school in the contrasting white limestone elements with American classicism of the twentieth-century

Eatman's North Carolina heritage is evident in the family heirlooms in his bedroom.

Georgian manner in the red-brick facade. Beers had arrived in Washington from Fairfield, Connecticut, in 1904, to spend the last seven years of his life designing seventy-one apartment buildings and town house developments for Harry Wardman works that encompassed a stylistic portfolio ranging from the American and European formalism popular in early-twentieth-century America, to more eclectic works drawing on American vernacular traditions and arts and crafts and Mediterranean motifs.

For the Dresden, Wardman and Beers carefully chose an agreeable, conventional classicism, developed to appeal to the conservative tastes of affluent couples and unmarried or widowed professionals. Expressed in the limestone base of broad arched windows and brick upper stories etched with limestone quoins, there is complete restraint in the structure's massing, alignment, and design. Indeed, Wardman built these apartments for the reserved individual or couple, established and comfortable. As renters, they might be military officers, political appointees, or diplomatic staff, or perhaps retirees temporarily living in the area. Beers designed elaborate and expensive parquet floors and plaster details in apartments, and marble inlay in the entrance lobby — craftsmanship and materials matched by few apartment houses in Washington.

Wardman made millions crafting his apartments, town houses, and single-

Decorations in the library include a portrait of Jeremy the terrier.

family subdivisions designed to capture just the clientele he desired. Like many successful developers, he had the ability to predict buyers' and renters' reactions to certain styles, materials, and interior designs before construction workers laid even the first foundation stone. That is why he had his own company architect; he was not interested in commissioning individual architects for each building, who then would move on to the next job, passing on Wardman's real estate instincts to competitors.

The Dresden opened in 1910 with fifty-seven spacious apartments of one, two, three, and four bedrooms on seven floors. It converted to condominium ownership in 1974, when many residents chose to buy rather than give up their glorious views across Rock Creek Park or the Washington Cathedral silhouetted against a colorful sky at sunset or the snow-covered Rock Creek Bridge; flower

beds in the rear courtyard in early spring; or the Dresden's subtle, trapezoidal rooms created by the curve of the avenue.

Helen McCain Smith, a resident of four decades, counts among the Dresden's notables. She was the secretary to First Lady Pat Nixon and to the Court of St. James under Anne Armstrong and Elliott Richardson. Princess Julia Grant Cantacuzen, another personality, arrived into this world in 1876 in her grandfather Ulysses S. Grant's White House (as her father fought in the Indian Wars in the West). She married Prince Michael Cantacuzen of St. Petersburg, Russia, where they lived before the Revolution and their exile in Sweden. The widowed princess returned to her native Washington in 1934 to live a quiet, elegant existence in the Dresden. Perhaps George Eatman, who bought his two-bedroom, sixth-floor residence in 1983, is most typical of the Dresden's contemporary community: middle-aged, accomplished, semi-retired, someone who takes great joy in renovation, antiques, original artworks, international travel, and evenings with a close society of friends.

In the library the understated classicism of the exterior (overleaf) is heightened by elaborate parquet floors, plaster detailing, oversized moldings, and columns. George Eatman painted the faux-bois and faux-marbre details himself. The sleigh bed was rescued from a shipwreck off the Outer Banks of North Carolina.

Apartments at the Dresden, originally a rental building, were of generous proportions, appealing to the individual or family generally accustomed to living in a house. The developer Harry Wardman made a fortune building apartments and single-family houses in the Washington area. One of the first to build for and market to a specific clientele, he changed the face of the city.

THE ALTAMONT

1916 | *Arthur Heaton, Architect*
George Truesdale, Builder

In Darryl Carter's apartment in the Altamont, the living room opens into the dining room. The sun porch (above) was a luxurious touch included in the original design.

WHILE FEW TURN-OF-THE-CENTURY OBSERVATION DECKS REMAIN IN SUCH VERTICAL METROPOLISES AS NEW YORK AND SAN FRANCISCO, IN WASHINGTON, A HORIZONTAL CITY WHERE VISTAS ARE HIGHLY VALUED AND CAREFULLY GUARDED, RESIDENTS HAVE PRESERVED THEIR HISTORIC LOOK-OUTS. INDEED, EXCEPTIONAL PANORAMIC VIEWS FROM EXCEPTIONAL BUILDINGS BESTOW A CERTAIN STATURE ON WASHINGTON PLACES. THE CATALOGUE OF SUCH SITES IS EXTENSIVE AND INCLUDES THE PRESIDENTIAL QUARTERS OF THE WHITE HOUSE, THE SPEAKER OF THE HOUSE OF REPRESENTATIVES'S OFFICES IN THE CAPITOL, THE FEDERAL RESERVE CHAIRMAN'S DINING ROOM, COVETED WATERGATE SUITES, AND THE NATIONAL CATHEDRAL'S BELL TOWER.

The elegant Altamont rises eighty-five feet from the high ground of tree-lined Wyoming Avenue, standing the equivalent of twenty-six stories above sea level. Two summer pavilions grace the rooftop terrace and open to scenes of the Capitol, the Potomac River, and Rock Creek Park. On a clear day, the Virginia hills unfold at the horizon.

Ceremonial lobbies, high ceilings, marble and plaster moldings in spacious rooms, and great views defined Washington's high-end apartment buildings in the 1910s. The Altamont's builder, Colonel George Truesdale, went to great lengths to pick out the right combination of architectural features—Italian Renaissance styling framed by Indiana limestone at the base, red tiles on the roof, and Roman yellow bricks across the face; marble fireplaces in all apartments, sunrooms in the largest; the Tudor style entrance hall vaulted to the ornately frescoed ceiling. Truesdale, who had acquired a healthy distaste for the long hallways in most large rental buildings of his day, vowed that the Altamont would instead offer "the exclusion and privacy of a well-appointed, private house."

Rather than lowering the ceilings to accommodate an additional rental floor, Truesdale instructed his architect, Arthur Heaton, to design apartments with ten-foot ceilings. For Truesdale and other luxury apartment builders, like Harry Wardman at the Dresden across Connecticut Avenue, decisions about how to draw affluent renters ultimately came down to a short list of "haves" and "have-nots." The "haves" included hotel-type services—barbers, billiards, ballrooms, cafes, and in-house cleaners. The Altamont's top floor housed a billiard room, an open loggia for canopied outdoor lounging and entertaining, and a private cafe for residents, patronized principally by Colonel Truesdale. It soon became a "have-not" and closed within five years.

Heaton, himself a Washington native who had apprenticed with local architects before traveling to Paris to study for a year at the Sorbonne, had absorbed the tastes of Washingtonians by firsthand observation. He excelled as a designer of residences. He also prospered as a versatile builder's architect of more than a thousand projects, gaining a reputation for working amicably with large commercial clients like Shannon & Luchs, the Chevy Chase Land

Although it is nearly a hundred feet above the streets of Kalorama Triangle, the kitchen gives every impression of being in a sophisticated country house in southern France.

View of the hall from the dining room (above) and the hallway, looking toward the round entrance foyer and the living room (opposite). The Altamont had the added luxury of marble fireplaces in larger apartments, and French doors. Multiple hallways allowed guests and servants to pass within the apartment and still maintain privacy.

Company, and the National Geographic Society's Gilbert Grosvenor, mostly on residences and institutional buildings. The majority of Heaton's work between 1900 and 1950 leaned toward proper Beaux-Arts and neo-Georgian influences, such as his design for the Park-and-Shop center on Connecticut Avenue, and the National Geographic Society's building on Fifteenth Street. The Altamont's romantic styling may well have shown Colonel Truesdale's preferences.

In time, the Altamont evolved into a small urban village, not so much the result of its communal billiard and dining rooms, but rather because of its mix of a modest number of apartments on each of the six floors and its conversion to cooperative ownership in 1949. Over eight decades, the Altamont has remained a pleasant residence in a pleasant urban neighborhood north of Dupont Circle, mostly devoid of celebrity residents and eccentric scandals. Most Altamont residents are Washingtonians, an eclectic community of young professionals, attorneys and self-made entrepreneurs, a few artists, and several retirees living a peaceful existence in the heart of downtown Washington.

Current Altamont resident Darryl Carter, a native Washingtonian and graduate of Georgetown University's Law School, manages his family's waste-management and chemical-transportation company. In 1993, he spent nearly a year renovating his residence. The design was his own creation, centered around a knowing respect for the Altamont's history and for the architectural integrity of its turn-of-the-century spaces.

In between daily business and renovation projects for family and friends, Carter maintains an active commitment to the city where he has lived all his life and a love for the heritage of Washington's residential buildings and neighborhoods. He shares this sensitivity with many of his neighbors, who value living in the historic Altamont and the urban Kalorama Triangle neighborhood.

DAVID SCHWARZ HOUSE

1925 | *Ewing & Allen*
Renovated 1986–87 | *David Schwarz*

The square entry foyer balances Ewing & Allen's 1925 classical architecture with the art deco and moderne styles of David Schwarz's 1987 renovation. The restored white marble floor with a black border complements the art deco bronze hanging lamp and statues of Greek gods Zeus and Orion framing the French doors. The house centers around this hall, which links the front double entrance doors to the terraced Roman garden and lily pond beyond.

THIS ELEGANT, NEOCLASSICAL-STYLE VILLA HAS LONG BEEN ASSOCIATED WITH MAJOR PATRONS OF THE BUILDING ARTS IN WASHINGTON. IN 1925 GERMAN-BORN CHRISTIAN HEURICH, A GENEROUS PHILANTHROPIST WHO CREATED THE CITY'S LARGEST BREWERY AND BUILT HIS OWN ROMANESQUE MANSION ON NEW HAMPSHIRE BELOW DUPONT CIRCLE (NOW THE COLUMBIA HISTORICAL SOCIETY OF WASHINGTON) COMMIS-SIONED NEW YORK ARCHITECTS EWING & ALLEN TO DESIGN THIS ITALIANATE REVIVAL RESIDENCE. THE HOUSE WAS HEURICH'S WEDDING PRESENT FOR HIS DAUGHTER AND HER HUSBAND, COLONEL GEORGE B. MCCLELLAN, THE GRANDSON OF CIVIL WAR GENERAL GEORGE B. MCCLELLAN.

In the dining room a traditional marble fireplace is juxtaposed with contemporary chairs and fine early-twentieth-century Viennese secessionist furniture and art nouveau silver candlesticks. This room, like all other principal rooms on the main floor, opens onto the terraced garden through arched French doors.

A bronze statue of the general overlooks Connecticut Avenue from the top of the hill at Columbia Road.

Mrs. McClellan lived here until her death in the late 1970s. She bequeathed the house to Washington's premier all-girls' school, Mount Vernon College, which occupied it as a dormitory. In 1986, architect David Schwarz acquired and completely renovated the three-story house as his own home.

Schwarz's award-winning designs and renovations have earned him an international reputation. His career began at Yale University, where he studied under Charles Moore, Cesar Pelli, and Vincent Scully, and continues to thrive thanks to the creativity, business savvy, and solid client relationships for which he is well known.

Schwarz completed his first Washington renovation in the Mount

Pleasant area in the mid-1970s, at a time, he says, "when my greatest occupation was sitting on the front steps drinking beer with fellow renovators who lived in the neighborhood." A decade later, by now a successful architect with offices in Washington and Fort Worth, as well as a private jet for shuttling among clients, he bought the former McClelland house. He and his office restyled the interior, fusing traditional and contemporary impulses. (Designers in his office have meritocratic involvement in every other commission, but Schwarz unapologetically admits that they had "absolutely no license with this house.")

From the outside the residence resembles an aging Italian palazzo with a flat slate roof and stucco weathered to a grayish hue. Grand arched casement windows dominate the street facade, while wide terra-cotta eaves crumble at the edges, a charming suggestion of the streets of Siena. When Ewing & Allen designed the house in the mid-1920s, turn-of-the-century Beaux-Arts refinement had given way to a revived interest among designers and patrons for neocolonial traditions in Georgian, French, Spanish, and Mediterranean styles. The house splays horizontally across a generous quarter-acre lot within this tight urban neighborhood. The long front facade with its double-door entranceway has always faced inward, to the side of the lot toward the driveway; and the narrower, secondary side elevation faces California Street. A terraced Roman garden grows easily around a fountain and lily pond along the rear facade.

Inside, the 6,500-square-foot steel-frame mansion is equipped with an elevator and only a few large rooms—a house built for a couple who needed a great deal of help. Perhaps too small for a larger family (only one principal bedroom) or a society couple (no grand stairway), for Schwarz, it possesses large spaces and all the right basics: living room, dining room, large kitchen, library, study, bedroom, and a great garden. After reworking the floor plan

The double living room showcases Schwarz's superb collection of twentieth-century furniture and architectural prints. Restored round-arched casements with Parisian brass hardware complement the new oak parquet floor and period style wall molding.

Club chairs from the liner **Ile de France** *are the center-piece of the double living room and of Schwarz's collection, lending a bold and sleek ambiance to the restrained classicist architecture.*

slightly to open up smaller spaces, Schwarz created a deco-influenced design scheme in which each room builds into the overall elegance of a monochromatic palette of black and white.

The restrained classicist architecture complements Schwarz's original deco and moderne furniture. His superb collection of twentieth-century art and architectural prints lends a mellow, noir ambiance to rooms and hallways. The traditional architecture combined with the deco decor of the Schwarz renovation is best revealed in the spare entry hall, a perfectly square room that extends the width of the house, front to back. Classic faux-marble pilasters framing the four walls create an atmosphere of elegant occasion, an architectural environment rich in subtle reference. The original white marble floor with a black border remains; an art deco bronze hanging lamp and statues of archetypal Greek gods Zeus and Orion frame the French doors.

The foyer opens to the double parlor on one side and to the formal dining room on the other. In the parlor, the restored fireplace mantel and the round-arched casements with Parisian brass hardware complement the new oak parquet floor and Schwarz's 1922 *Ile de France* ocean liner chairs. The formal dining room adjoins the everyday dining room, where Schwarz enjoys dinner with friends and breakfast with his partner. The second floor also has few rooms: a book-lined oak library, a small home office, and the master bedroom and bath, which extends out to a terrazzo patio overlooking the garden.

Because of the McClellans' unique requirements (the colonel was a paraplegic), there was no main stairway in this otherwise formal house. There was only a narrow service stair for maids, nurses, and butlers, which did not even meet the city's fire code standards. Schwarz enlarged the stairwell for ease and safety, and on the third floor (which he gutted to remove eleven servants' rooms, replacing them with guest rooms) he created a large skylight through which sunlight streams down the stairwell.

It is interesting that for an architect who enjoys the individualism of innovation, traditional principles form the core of his design work. "I continue to learn, to look at buildings, to look at books," he explains. "It is design by discovery." In the end, David Schwarz believes that vibrancy in buildings and vibrancy on the street are the twin goals of good design, whether the project involves renovating a historic building or designing a new structure. As his own residence demonstrates, with its conserved exterior and altered interior that respects the collective relationship of buildings, sidewalks, and streetscape to the people who use them, the primary objective is neighborhood preservation.

BRITISH AMBASSADOR'S RESIDENCE

1925–30 | *Sir Edwin Landseer Lutyens*

The gallery of the British ambassador's residence on Massachusetts Avenue connects private and public rooms through the length of the house. The floor of polished white Vermont marble and black Pennsylvania slate leads from the ambassador's library at the east end, continues past the ballroom, the family's morning room, the main drawing room, and dining room, to the garden door on the west end.

BRITISH AMBASSADORS MAY COME AND GO, YET THE AMBASSADOR'S RESIDENCE ON MASSACHUSETTS AVENUE REMAINS THE SYMBOL OF THE UNITED KINGDOM IN WASHINGTON. THIS GRACIOUS COUNTRY HOUSE WAS THE HOME OF SIR JOHN AND LADY ELIZABETH KERR THROUGH 1997, THEIR EASY WARMTH FILLING THE ROOMS AND HALLWAYS. THE KERRS' WEDDING CHINA ADORNED THE MANTELS, AND LADY KERR HERSELF RESTORED THE WOOD PANELING IN THE AMBASSADOR'S LIBRARY. OF THE DOZENS OF FOREIGN EMBASSIES AND CONSULATES IN WASHINGTON, THIS ONE IS AMONG THE LARGEST AND MOST PUBLIC, SERVING FOR MORE THAN SEVEN DECADES THE MANY PURPOSES OF HOME,

hall, and stage set. Few weeks go by that are not filled with dinners, luncheons, and teas.

"In the whole country there is no such stately function as dinner at the British Embassy," Larz Anderson, a one-time ambassador to Japan, said in 1933. "The tall footmen in royal liveries that line the wide stairways and serve the dinner, and especially the kilted Scotch guardsman in the gallery make the guest realize that he is in a foreign country." The proper hospitality of Sir Ronald and Lady Elizabeth Lindsay, who represented the British Empire in Washington through the 1930s, earned this rare encomium from Anderson, whose mansion stood nearby on Massachusetts Avenue. King George V would have had it no other way. It was on his birthday in 1928 that architect Sir Edwin Lutyens laid the cornerstone of the house and chancery (his monogram, GVR, is carved in the residence's limestone trim and all fireplace flues).

By the 1920s, Massachusetts Avenue held sway as Washington's gold coast, having developed over five decades into a shaded promenade of stunning stone mansions and handsome brick town houses. Most of the embassy's neighbors were houses of socialites, millionaires, entrepreneurs, or diplomats. Only a few foreign consulates had moved into older, nineteenth-century houses south of Dupont Circle. Britain's choice of this northernmost four-acre site proved to be farsighted. The ministry had acquired the property near Observatory Circle in 1925 from developer Harry W. Wardman, who had made his name building major residential projects (such as the Dresden on Connecticut Avenue) in the District's wooded northern reaches. In addition to cash, Wardman also received title to the embassy's old chancery on Connecticut Avenue at N Street, which had become a choice commercial address by 1930.

The British ministry admittedly intended to fit in with the avenue's public show of private wealth, but the Georgian style residence, with its high-topped chimney stacks, instead set off a whole new trend. "Embassy Row" emerged after 1928, accelerated by various economic forces. The stock market crashed the year after construction started, property taxes escalated, and higher and higher maintenance costs for new domestic technology pressed the newly taxed finances of massive Massachusetts Avenue houses. Within the decade, this grand residential avenue would become a more practical address for foreign embassies and consulates.

The ambassador's private library is an elegant room paneled in rich honey-toned wood with fluted Corinthian pilasters and a cove ceiling to emphasize its height. Lady Kerr restored the library in 1995.

The House of Windsor's choice of Lutyens to design the United Kingdom's representative residence in America was an interesting one. Britons apparently sought the domestic image only Lutyens could create. The greatest English architect of his generation, he produced well over three hundred houses as well as both small and monumental buildings across England, Ireland, Belgium, France, India, and South Africa. It was his special rapport with clients that secured him hundreds of patrons. "There will never be great architects or great architecture without great patrons," he noted in 1915. Indeed, many of his clients defined the essence of Edwardian society in the early decades of the twentieth century, and included Jennie Churchill and Vita Sackville-West. The ambassador's residence is the only building Lutyens designed in the United States, a regrettable fact for his admirers on this side of the Atlantic. He was thoroughly ensconced in Edwardian England and apparently cultivated no American clients.

Lutyens's personal design style brilliantly combined the romantic and classical aspects of English architecture with large-scale proportions and subtle transitions to establish a clear hierarchy of spaces. His sense of mass and volume was similar to that of the great American architect of the same generation, John

Russell Pope. As one enters the British ambassador's house, the flow of the double-flying arches moves one through the entranceway and up the grand staircase. The main corridor connects formal and informal, private and public rooms through the 167-foot length of the house. The floor of polished white Vermont marble and black Pennsylvania slate leads from the ambassador's library at one end, down to the ballroom, the garden portico, and the family's morning room, past the main drawing room on one side and the state dining room on the other, then outdoors to the herb and fruit garden at the west end, and beyond to Lutyens's unusual raised pool terrace. The architect's whimsical hand appears in the human faces and endearing animals rendered on such small but meaningful details as shutter holds and fireplace mantels, as well as the stone lions and unicorns poised to welcome guests at the entrance gateways.

In its overall plan, this house bears a certain resemblance to the palatial Viceroy's House in New Delhi, which Lutyens was simultaneously designing for the British foreign ministry. Here in this urban setting, he created a fine-scaled country house, choosing an exterior of Pennsylvania-fired red brick and very American features drawn from the colonial architecture of Williamsburg and rural Virginia. The ambassador's residence was designed and built with chancery offices but the expanding diplomatic staff outgrew the space by the early 1950s, and moved out of the house into a new six-story office building next door. With the chancery then in a separate building, the ministry renovated the vacated space in the house into suites for visiting ministers and apartments for the ambassador's staff.

The house endures with its adaptability to the changing needs and customs of the ambassadors' families, who have found domestic comfort in the library, the breakfast and morning rooms, and upstairs bedrooms all named for ambassadors: Sir Howard, Sir Lindsay, Sir Dean, the Marquess of Lothian, and Lords Inverchapel, Franks, Sherfield, Caccia, and Harleck. The Palladian style private library is especially rich and warm in its natural, honey-toned wood. Fluted Corinthian pilasters are placed in perfect symmetry around the room. Just down the hall, by contrast, the ballroom and north portico open up for official entertaining. Lutyens crafted the portico with giant pillars standing out to the rose garden in the colonial manner because, as he discovered on his first visit to America in 1925, "we are near plantation country." On balmy spring and fall evenings, Sir John and Lady Elizabeth would enjoy private dinners on the portico. The Marquess of Lothian, ambassador from 1939 to 1941 and an avid gardener, had acquired the public park adjacent to the residence in 1939 to protect the property's borders and give future ambassadors the gift of a vast rose garden. And when it is in full bloom, there is no lovelier invitation in town than to a reception at the British ambassador's residence for strawberries and cream and champagne on the lawn.

Lutyens designed the portico with giant pillars in the colonial manner because, as he observed on his first visit to the site, "We are near plantation country." The vast rose garden, cultivated by the Marquess of Lothian, today is a laboratory of American Beauties.

BELGIAN AMBASSADOR'S RESIDENCE

1931 | *Horace Trumbauer*

The gallery (above) connects the grand reception rooms, one flowing into the next, from the dining room at one end, to the grand salon, the library, and the garden room at the southern end. The oak-paneled library (left) was modeled after a room that is now installed at the Metropolitan Museum of Art in New York.

DOUBLE ENTENDRES SURROUND THIS HOUSE, BUILT IN 1931 BY AUTOMOTIVE HEIRESS DELPHINE DODGE AND HER SPECULATOR HUSBAND, RAYMOND BAKER. THE ROCOCO-STYLED LIMESTONE VILLA DUPLICATES AN EIGHTEENTH-CENTURY LANDMARK IN PARIS, THE CITY THAT STOOD AS WASHINGTON'S ARCHITECTURAL IDEAL. SINCE 1944, THIS HOUSE, THE MOST AUTHENTICALLY FRENCH BUILDING IN WASHINGTON, HAS BEEN HOME TO THE UNITED STATES AMBASSADOR FROM BELGIUM, THE NATION IRONICALLY POSSESSED OF A LOVE-HATE RELATIONSHIP WITH FRANCE. THESE TWO OWNERS HAVE PRIDED THEIR ROLES AS STEWARDS OF HERITAGE OVER THE SIX DECADES SINCE PHILADELPHIA ARCHITECT

The grand salon, the center-piece of the residence's public rooms, is paneled in blue and gold boiserie. Natural light and vast space are enhanced by French doors opening out to the slate terrace and breathtaking views across the Potomac River and the Blue Ridge Mountains beyond. The interior remains much the same as it was in its original 1931 design, when Edouard Hitau, of the house of Lucien Alvaoine and Cie in Paris, designed the formal rooms for Delphine and Raymond Baker.

Philadelphia architect Horace Trumbauer designed the Baker residence on Foxhall Road, yet each has been motivated by different architectural impulses. The Bakers adored the richness of French buildings. The Belgians revere the grandeur of history and are mildly amused by the grandiosity of the Baker-Dodge imprint.

While marital peace seemed elusive, the Bakers well understood the social strength of fine architecture. Members of Delphine's family actually kept Trumbauer's office quite busy during the 1920s and 1930s with the design of residences in Michigan, Washington, and New York, so it is no surprise that her mother asked the architect to design her daughter's Washington residence. Essentially, it was intended to replicate the Hotel Rothelin de Charolais in Paris, designed by Lassurance.

While this might seem sheer mimicry from the hand of a well-regarded society architect, the stature of Trumbauer's portfolio rested on reproductions of eighteenth-century classic French landmarks rather than the twentieth-century neoclassicism of his contemporaries. This is exactly why his wealthy clientele sought him out. In Washington, Trumbauer also designed the Ritz Carlton Hotel on Massachusetts Avenue (now the Sheraton International), and advised French architect Etienne Sanson in designing Perry Belmont's house on New Hampshire Avenue. Indeed, the social pedigree of the Baker-Trumbauer collaboration continued even after the Baker household dissolved. Raymond Baker died in 1935. Delphine Dodge promptly married her third husband, and her mother-in-law by her first marriage, Mrs. Edward Townsend Stotesbury of Palm Beach, had moved into this house and named the house Marly, after Louis XIV's country retreat. At Mrs. Stotesbury's death, in 1944, the Belgian government bought the house.

What Trumbauer may have lacked in originality he made up for in the residence's superb placement on the highland of Foxhall Road. Gracefully set back against a circular drive on a twelve-acre wooded site, the residence enjoys privacy amid thick stands of evergreen and boxwood, and affords spectacular views westward across the Potomac River and the Blue Ridge Mountains beyond. The aura of intimacy and charm realized here was just the environment the aristocratic hotels in Paris emphasized in the early 1700s. The long symmetrical facade centers on the pedimented entrance with arched windows and a decorous carved frieze of cupids embracing roses. The floral theme continues inside. Flowers fill the house, from the urns in the drive, to the grand salon with a wall of French doors opening out to a terrace of roses, geraniums, and hibiscus, to the garden solarium at the south end, still used by Ambassador Andre and Danielle Adam as the summer sleeping room and still hung with the Bakers' paintings of cockatoos, flamingos, spoonbills, and macaws.

The Adams, like other ambassadors before them who come for four-year tours, have added personal touches in treasured antiques and old French chemist jars, especially in the most comfortable of rooms, the mellowed oak library. The interior design remains much the same as it was in 1931, when Parisian Edouard Hitau, of the house of Lucien Alavoine and Cie, designed the formal rooms. He returned for Mrs. Stotesbury in 1935, and again for Belgium's first envoy in 1945.

At once gracious and ceremonial, the Belgian ambassador's residence beholds a lifestyle that few people today (even in Washington) can imagine—or afford. Even for Belgium's most visited embassy in the world, host to 3,500 guests each year and the temporary home of visiting ministers and diplomats, the original live-in staff of fourteen has today diminished to an economical five: chef, chamber maid, laundress, gardener, and chauffeur. Still, the setting, the view, and the damp weathered stone draw one so easily into an imaginary era when wealthy Washingtonians pondered the fate of America over champagne and cigars.

The Belgian Ambassador's
residence is closely patterned
on the Hôtel de Rothelein in
Paris of 1700, designed by
Pierre Lassurance, who was
Jules Hardouin Mausart's
chief assistant during
the design of the Palace
of Versailles.

PRIVATE
WASHINGTON
136

JOHN & KATHRINE FOLGER HOUSE

1935–36 | *John Russell Pope*
Landscape Design 1942–45 | *Rose Greeley*

The library of the Folger house, designed in 1935 by John Russell Pope, was a wedding gift to John and Kathrine Folger and now is owned by their son and daughter-in-law, John and Juliet Folger.

KATHRINE DULIN OF KNOXVILLE, TENNESSEE, GREW UP IN A HOUSE DESIGNED BY THE EMINENT NEW YORK ARCHITECT JOHN RUSSELL POPE. IN 1910 HER FATHER HAD COMMISSIONED POPE TO DESIGN CRESCENT BLUFF, THE ARCHITECT'S FIRST RESIDENCE IN THE STATE OF TENNESSEE. YEARS LATER, WHEN KATHRINE MARRIED JOHN CLIFFORD FOLGER, THE SON OF AN APPLE FARMER FROM PULLMAN, WASHINGTON, HER FATHER GAVE THEM A WEDDING PRESENT OF A NEW HOUSE BY POPE, THIS ONE IN WASHINGTON, D.C. HERE CLIFF FOLGER ESTABLISHED THE INVESTMENT BANKING FIRM OF FOLGER, NOLAN, FLEMING, DOUGLAS IN THE DOWNTOWN FINANCIAL DISTRICT, WHERE THE FIRM OWNS A HANDSOME BEAUX-ARTS STYLE BUILDING.

The newlyweds' belated gift of a residence set them up in the style to which Kathrine was accustomed. Yet it was "a relatively small house for Pope," noted the architect's biographer, Stephen Bedford, and it was designed rather quickly in 1935. Pope was by then well known in Washington's political, artistic, and social circles. Twenty years before, President Woodrow Wilson had appointed him to a five-year seat on the prestigious Commission of Fine Arts. His designs for monumental buildings located at the primary axials around the Mall endowed official Washington with a lasting imprint of classicist refinement, notably the vast National Archives on Pennsylvania Avenue, the DAR's Constitution Hall, and his last and greatest landmarks, the Jefferson Memorial and the National Gallery of Art. Pope's influence also touched private Washington with major manses for notable residents Robert and Kathrine McCormick on Massachusetts Avenue and the Henry Whites and Irwin B. Laughlins, both on Crescent Place in the Meridian Hill neighborhood.

Pope, who moved easily among the highest ranks of New York and Washington societies, had enjoyed an impeccable education in classic architecture. He distinguished himself with an artist's eye for the drama of great spaces and large proportions, and a personal graciousness that disarmed even the most self-important clients. Early in his career, as with most young architects who came of age at the turn of the century, Pope was a practitioner of ancient and traditional styles of Rome, France, Greece, and England. A graduate of Columbia University's architecture program, he traveled through Europe while studying at the American Academy in Rome and the Ecole des Beaux-Arts in Paris. In 1903, at age twenty-nine, Pope opened his own practice in New York.

The power of Pope's buildings rises out of the quiet aura created by his reductionist use of ornament, applied against large-scale classical orders. His academic training prepared him to develop an ideology of material beauty, expressed through traditional architecture. His artistic talent enabled him to use architectural forms in ways that produced a particular emotional environment appropriate to a given place, whether it was a residence, memorial, museum, or public hall. The Jefferson Memorial is remembered for its quiet reverence, the National Gallery for the deep respect shown the artworks, the Folger house for its sense of domestic calm.

The Folger residence was a very private commission by Pope and Washington standards. The reserved, some might say plain classicism defers to the young family of four: Kathrine, Cliff, and their two sons, John and Lee. While Pope was working with the Folgers, the sixty-one-year-old architect was terminally ill. During the last two years of his life he made frequent day trips from New York to Washington, as he was also designing the Jefferson Memorial and the National Gallery of Art for his patron Andrew Mellon. As the Folger house rose from foundation level to eaves, Pope took the time at the end of demanding days to stop at the Folger house in the upper Kalorama neighborhood before returning to Union Station to board the New York–bound train. Through it all, Pope's close associate Otto Eggers worked with Kathrine Folger on the final details. Eggers remained a family friend after Pope's death in 1937, returning often to take care of touch-up details.

Cliff Folger shrewdly moved his wife and two young boys into their unfinished house in 1936 to get the workmen out. The family bedded down in sleeping bags in the playroom atop of the garage, but they soon settled into a comfortable existence, Cliff walking downtown each day to manage his firm, the boys off to private schools, and Kathrine finishing the house and laying out

The dining room exemplifies the refinement of Pope's classicism in his reductionist use of ornament applied against finely scaled classical orders and moldings — the fireplace, window cornices, and the built-in china nook. The elegant dining room, with a stripped oak floor and ten-foot ceiling, is a space for formal occasions; the adjacent living room, extending the full length of the house, accommodates grand entertaining.

the gardens, buying additional lots between Cleveland Avenue and Woodland Drive. Pope had oriented all of the principal rooms toward the outdoors, creating a country-house setting in the city, as he did in most of his Washington houses. A wall of French doors along all the ground-floor rooms opened to the south garden. Throughout the year, the living room, dining room, and library, as well as the family's bedrooms on the second floor, were bathed in natural light.

This brick residence with white neo-Grec trim is marked by familiar Pope touches. Rooms are scaled to match their purpose and hierarchical importance, openly spacious with ten-foot ceilings, and finished with stripped oak floors and carved marble facing all fireplaces. The living room, the largest and grandest room for entertaining, extends the full length of the house, front to back, opening out to the terraced garden. The dining room, the most elegant in classic trim, remains the space of formal occasions. The original kitchen revealed the architect's and Kathrine's limited firsthand knowledge of food preparation. When her daughter-in-law Juliet C. Folger of Designs East & West restored the house in 1993, she and consulting architect Richard Williams of Williams & Dykeman reconfigured the kitchen area to open up circulation and provide practical spaces for large-scale entertaining.

Kathrine may not have been a natural cook, but she was an avid organizer, planning events and fund-raisers for the Washington Cathedral and the American Cancer Society, as well as her husband's Republican party functions as national finance chairman during Dwight D. Eisenhower's reelection campaign in 1956. While Cliff served as ambassador to Belgium during 1957 and 1958, Kathrine played to her strength as a diplomatic hostess extraordinaire. Even better, her annual Azalea Tea highlighted Washington's spring social calendar for three decades since the 1960s. She carefully scheduled the event around the blossoming of her famed Azalea Walk, designed and planted in 1942 by landscape architect Rose Greeley. Mrs. Greeley and Kathrine built the garden sequentially, as money became available, extending the original flagstone terrace and adding a brick wall around the entire property line to create the sense of a country estate in the city. The rest of the family joined in Kathrine's out-of-doors enthusiasm, and life at the Folger house from April through October was lived largely outside, on the lawns and terrace, amid the garden and azaleas.

Today, the Folger residence seems a continuum of its own history. More than sixty years after it was built, it remains the mother ship of the Folger family, maintained by Kathrine and Cliff's youngest son, Lee, now senior partner of Folger Nolan. The Folger house, notably, is John Russell Pope's only Washington residence still occupied as a private home. The others, more spacious and expensive to maintain, have passed to institutional owners such as Meridian House International and the Embassy of Brazil. This formerly "modest" house for Pope is now revered for its provenance and private residency.

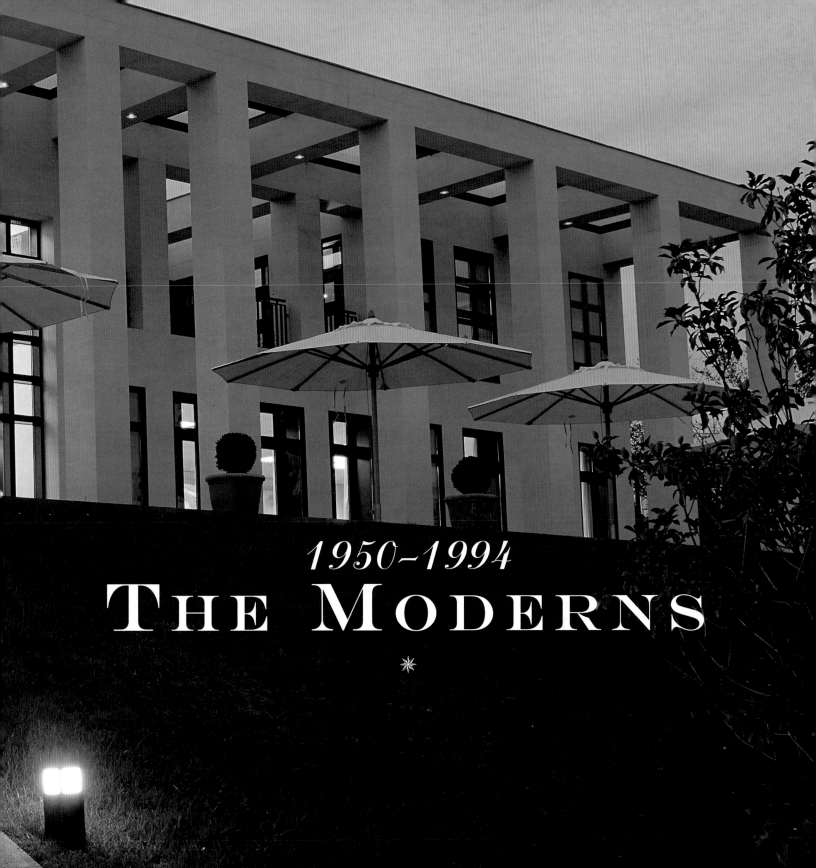

1950–1994
THE MODERNS

✳

SAM GILLIAM &
ANNIE GAWLAK HOUSE

1950 | *Owner-Builder*
Renovated **1997** | *Mary Drysdale*

Artist Sam Gilliam and curator Annie Gawlak bought this nondescript 1950s builder's house precisely for its renovation possibilities. With friend and designer Mary Drysdale, they created the light- and color-filled dining room around Gilliam's vast mural and impasto-painted office chairs (a signature design) and fluted classical columns.

WHEN THE PAINTER SAM GILLIAM SETTLED IN WASHINGTON IN 1962, HE HAD ALREADY GIVEN UP ON THE IDEA OF AN ARTISTIC CAREER. "IT LOOKED TOTALLY IMPOSSIBLE," HE SAYS TODAY, AS THE MAINSTREAM SENTIMENT DURING THE 1960S AND EARLY 1970S WAS THAT "NO BLACK ARTIST WORTH HIS SALT WOULD PAINT ABSTRACT ART." GILLIAM BECAME A TEACHER, YET WASHINGTON'S THRIVING ARTISTS' COMMUNITY, NOTABLY TOM DOWNING, HOWARD MIRIAM, AND BRITON MORRIS, INSPIRED HIM TO PAINT LATE INTO THE NIGHT AND ON WEEKENDS. HIS FIRST SHOWINGS, IN 1971 IN CHICAGO AND PARIS, LAUNCHED HIS CAREER; HE IS NOW AN INTERNATIONAL NAME IN THE ART WORLD.

Crossing the threshold of Sam Gilliam and Annie Gawlak's Rock Creek Park residence opens up a brilliant domestic world of light and color and art-filled vistas. The artist and his art curator partner complement one another in lively and interesting ways, as evidenced by the way they shared in the design and rebuilding of their home. Gilliam and Gawlak met in 1985; she was director of the Middendorf Gallery where Gilliam was exhibiting and he was living a bachelor's existence in his Lamont Street town house in Mount Pleasant. As their lives came together, Annie held fast to the bucolic vision of a home, a place surrounded by trees and a garden—not concrete sidewalks, neighbors two feet on either side, and a sliver of grass out back.

Their search for a makeover house was rewarded in 1996, as they drove around northwest neighborhoods on Sunday afternoons. Both spotted this 1950s ranch-style house on Quincy Street that had stood vacant and on the market for three years. Both the interior and the exterior looked every bit the

The rear hallway (opposite) reveals the couple's passion for mixing historic and contemporary vernacular and found objects. The breakfast room (above) integrates art and architecture with everyday living—Gawlak's wall piece of metal washers hanging on nails and Gilliam's toy collection and antique furniture.

cheaply built contractor-owner house it was, made out of lumber the contractor had or lumber he could get from job sites. "It is not a very intelligent house," Sam admits, not the design, structure, or interior plan. Yet the creative pair saw beyond the run-down exterior to the possibilities for high ceilings and free-flowing spaces inside, and a beautiful lot backing up to trees and woodland outside. Before they bought, however, Sam and Annie asked their friend and colleague, interior designer Mary Drysdale, to come and walk through the house, to see if she could envision even a glimmer of their ideas for remaking the house. Indeed, Drysdale saw much more.

The day they bought the Quincy Street house, Drysdale began demolishing interior walls and drop ceilings, leaving a shell that she painted white—floors, walls, and ceilings—an open,

The living room, a free-flowing space that looks out to a private reserve of Rock Creek Park woodland, is a personal gallery of Gilliam's art and that of friends and colleagues Tom Downing, Howard Mirian, and Briton Morris.

unifying tabula rasa. Ten days later, Sam and Annie moved in and they and Drysdale continued to shape, paint, and furnish this work in progress. For Drysdale, Sam and Annie are refreshing to work with; she especially appreciates their ease with major design decisions. As artists, they know they can undo and redo all over again. "It is so easy to work with people who are not intimidated by construction and deconstruction," Drysdale adds. Her approach to design focuses first on her clients' interests and activities and how these might be manifest in the way they live. With this, she says, "getting the plan right is absolutely key to good residential work." It is the relationship of spaces to one another, the flow, the vistas through and across spaces, and how these interact with the residents' character that are paramount. As for the design success of this working trio of artists, Drysdale explains, and Gilliam and Gawlak agree, that it's about reflecting personality: "It's not about the ownership of the idea," she says. "It's about the quality of the idea."

CHRIS & DEEDY OGDEN HOUSE

1885 | *Architect Unknown*
Renovated **1960** | *Hugh Newell Jacobson*

Architect Hugh Newell Jacobsen renovated an 1885 Georgetown Victorian into a modern residence in 1960 by adding an identical row house to one side and opening up the interior around a central garden atrium.

ARCHITECT HUGH NEWELL JACOBSEN, A DIS-CIPLE OF LOUIS KAHN AT YALE AND LATER AN ASSOCIATE OF PHILIP JOHNSON, OPENED HIS OWN OFFICE IN WASHINGTON IN 1956. IN 1960, BY WAY OF REFERRAL FROM ANOTHER ARCHITECT, HE WAS ASKED TO RENOVATE AN OLD HOUSE FOR PAINTER AND DEMOCRATIC PARTY ACTIVIST PHYLLIS (PHYZZIE) PRESTON AND HER JOURNALIST HUS-BAND, ROBERT E. LEE (KNOWN AS GENERAL TO HIS FRIENDS). FACED WITH A DARK AND NARROW VICTORIAN TOWN HOUSE, JACOBSEN HAD HIS WORK CUT OUT FOR HIM.

THE FORMIDABLE FINE ARTS COMMISSION, THE STEWARD OF HISTORIC GEORGETOWN AND FEDERAL WASHINGTON, REQUIRED THAT CHANGES

or additions to a front facade conform to the character of the original houses in the area. Thus Jacobsen's primary challenge in remaking the row house one of five typical Victorians in the heart of historic Georgetown, a few hundred feet from the eighteenth-century Dumbarton House and across the street from two of Downing and Vaux's romantic 1850s villas, was to remain true to his modernist principles and his clients' wishes.

To conform to the block's modest nineteenth-century scale, Jacobsen enlarged the house by adding an identical row house to its east. The front doorway, which he positioned between the two structures, opened to the twenty-one-foot glass-walled atrium and Phyzzie's orangerie overlooking the flagstone terrace and lily pool. Jacobsen completely redesigned the garden facade, which cannot be seen from the street, in the modern style. The restful lily and goldfish pond, a collaboration with landscape architect Lester Collins, anchors the full width of the terraced garden. To bring more light into the house, Jacobsen dropped the sill of the tall windows all around, creating floor-to-ceiling windows.

In 1960 Georgetown, this brash remodeling stunned a society unfamiliar with both modern design and the adaptation of historic buildings for contemporary use. The tall plate-glass windows with no cross mullions glaring out like vertical picture windows pressed the goodwill of the Fine Arts Commission, which had already extended its standards of acceptability quite far on this project. The Commission filed a condemnation notice, forcing Jacobsen to apply "flexy" mullions to create smaller window panes, which remain to this day.

Jacobsen makes few apologies for the drama and austerity of his interiors. "I design the house around the family," he asserts. "You should try to make people look the best you can in their own house." His exteriors, by contrast, tend toward traditional forms and conventional scales, concealing the impact of the interior and private outdoor spaces. In this house, the surprise happens as one steps across the front threshold and into the atrium, the centerpiece of the house.

For nearly three decades the Lees enjoyed a fascinating social milieu in their home. One friend recalled the frequent image of "Phyzzie opening the door, General at her elbow, standing there in a pool of light which seemed to be of her own making." Indeed, it was that remarkable "pool of light" from the atrium, Deedy Ogden remembers, that drew her and Chris to purchase the house in 1989. The Ogdens were returning from a tour in London, where Chris, a journalist and the author of best-selling biographies of Pamela Harriman and Walter Annenberg, headed *Time* magazine's London bureau, and Deedy ran an art gallery while working on her own paintings. They knew it was the right house for their family, with private upstairs rooms for each of their teenage children, and a quiet, sunlit den where Chris could write.

The Ogdens had come to appreciate modern design when they lived next door to Helmut Jahn in Chicago in the early 1970s. Now they live in flowing spaces amid Deedy's large oil paintings and an eclectic assortment of furnishings and personal collectibles gathered from around the globe—Tajik rugs from Central Asia, for example, and a religious chest from Thailand.

Jacobsen, who has designed houses throughout the world, has built only one other in Washington, and that was for himself. Conventional preferences appear to overwhelm architectural patrons here. Yet, what is more traditional than an architect whose principles are grounded in the essence of a particular place? "A house should look like a house," says Jacobsen. And indeed, the Ogden residence is a timeless object of historic Georgetown.

For the Ogdens, it was the remarkable "pool of light" in the atrium and the sunfilled rooms, like the living room (above) that drew Deedy and Chris to the house.

On the garden facade, the
house opens out from the
atrium into a shaded flagstone
terrace with a serene lily and
goldfish pond.

KREEGER HOUSE MUSEUM

1966–67 | *Philip Johnson*

Philip Johnson created this white travertine Eastern style palace based on ideas he garnered from a 1966 tour of Egypt and India, notably the spatial system of twenty-two-foot modules and the groin-vaulted dome roof.

The bronze sculpture, Pomona, cast in 1922 by Aristide Maillol, joins others by Henry Moore, Jean Arp, and Jacques Lipschitz standing serenely amid the pristine natural environment.

THIS RESIDENCE TURNED MUSEUM IS THE FORMER HOME OF DAVID AND CARMEN KREEGER, WHO BEQUEATHED THEIR COLLECTION OF ART, AS WELL AS THIS HOUSE, TO CREATE THE KREEGER MUSEUM. THOUGHTFULLY CONCEIVED BY THE KREEGERS, THE DESIGN FOR THE RESIDENCE WAS CAREFULLY EXECUTED BY ARCHITECT PHILIP JOHNSON. THE GRACEFUL TRAVERTINE PALACE THAT RESULTED WOULD MARK A CHANGE IN BOTH THE LOOK AND TECHNOLOGY OF AMERICAN MUSEUM ARCHITECTURE.

GEICO INSURANCE FOUNDER DAVID LLOYD KREEGER AND HIS WIFE, CARMEN, ACQUIRED A FIVE-AND-A-HALF-ACRE WOODED SITE AMID GENTLE HILLS AND VALLEYS ON FOXHALL ROAD

in the mid-1960s. The Kreegers had begun to collect seriously only a decade before they built this house, acquiring paintings by Courbet, Corot, Monet, Renoir, and Degas, then progressively moving toward more abstract and avant-garde work. They purchased Native African masks and figures, and paintings by Pierre Bonnard, Paul Cézanne, Frank Stella, Arshile Gorky, Max Beckmann, and Edvard Munch. By the time they retained Philip Johnson in 1966, the collection had become the focus of the Kreegers' lives and of Johnson's design concept for this residence: a home for the Kreegers and a gallery to display their magnificent art.

A controversial architect revered then and today for his energy and breadth, and criticized for the unevenness of his designs, Johnson served as the Museum of Modern Art's architect-in-residence during the 1960s; he completed the museum's east wing and sculpture garden in 1964. The

The Kreegers endowed
and bequeathed the
Foxhall Road house and
their extensive art collection
to create the Kreeger
Museum, which opened to
the public in 1994.

The Kreegers' collection of modern French art, including works by Claude Monet, Edgar Degas, Pierre Bonnard, Paul Cézanne, and the Russian-born Marc Chagall, is installed in the two-story central hall. The Kreegers also filled the hall on many occasions with the music of Isaac Stern, Pinchus Zukerman (with whom David Kreeger played his Stradivarius), Pablo Casals, and the Tokyo and Cleveland quartets.

Kreegers asked him to design their home in 1966, the same year Johnson embarked on a month-long tour of Egypt and India. Johnson's biographer, Franz Schulze, has maintained that the Eastern ideas Johnson absorbed from this trip dominated the design of the Kreeger residence, notably the architectural system of modular spaces and the groin-vaulted dome roof overhead, with a voluminous two-story central hall designed for exhibiting the Kreeger's modern French pieces. Yet Johnson had been a protégé of Bauhaus principals Walter Gropius and Marcel Breuer, and a rationalist approach to architecture, which was at times even classical in its expression (notably the AT&T Corporate Headquarters in New York, built two decades later), was deeply ingrained in him.

In this modern classical design, the central theme—art—intertwines with hierarchies of sub-themes—home, sculpture, light, garden. Johnson abided by classic principles in mathematical precision: the spatial system of twenty-two-foot square modules, the fine finishes of mitered corners and luminous Italian travertine (cut and numbered for on-site placement before shipping to the States), and the strong forms in the vaulted domes, bright art galleries, and enclosed family quarters. Outdoors, the pristine natural environment is amplified by bronze sculptures by Henry Moore, Jean Arp, and Jacques Lipschitz.

A constant dialogue exists between the art and the architecture. The art, it seems, fills the voids of the architecture. And the Kreegers filled the halls on many occasions with the music of Isaac Stern, Pinchus Zukerman (with whom David played his Stradivarius), Pablo Casals, and the Tokyo and Cleveland quartets.

The Kreegers had long planned to endow and bequeath the house and their art collection to create the Kreeger Museum. Their two children fully supported the museum in their parents' name and memory. David Lloyd Kreeger died in 1990, and Carmen moved to a smaller residence in 1992. The museum opened to the public in 1994, becoming a mecca for art connoisseurs, amateur and professional alike, even in this capital of museums. This role shift refocuses critical attention on Johnson's original design: the house has become even more controversial in a city of conventional architecture. Visitors passing through to admire the art primarily view the private residence as a cool, inhospitable environment. Yet beyond Johnson's precise design, the house possesses a very personal intimacy connected with the Kreegers' life together collecting art.

DENYCE GRAVES & DAVID PERRY HOUSE

1989 | *James Athey, Builder*

In their Leesburg, Virginia, home, opera diva Denyce Graves and her husband, musician David Perry, have re-created the color and drama of stage sets worldwide on which Ms. Graves has appeared.

THE VARIOUS HOMES THAT OPERA DIVA DENYCE GRAVES HAS OCCUPIED PUNCTUATE THE STORY OF A YOUNG AND REMARKABLE LIFE THAT HAS KNOWN POVERTY, MUSICAL SUCCESS, AND LONG HOURS OF HARD WORK SINGING, WAITRESSING, DISHWASHING, AND HOUSE-CLEANING. NOW, AT AGE THIRTY-THREE, SHE FULLY APPRECIATES THE COMFORT AND LUXURY SHE SHARES WITH HER HUSBAND, DAVID PERRY, A CLASSICAL GUITARIST AND TENOR, IN THEIR SPACIOUS NINETEEN-ROOM HOUSE. FAITH, FAMILY, TALENT, AND DISCIPLINE CONSTITUTE THE ARCHITECTURE OF HER PERSONAL VALUES. COLOR, DRAMA, AND SCENIC IMAGES MAKE UP THE ARCHITECTURE OF HER RESIDENCE.

Born and raised in the southwest district of Washington, Denyce grew up in a fatherless family of three children. From her native urban neighborhood, she went on a work-study scholarship to study at the elite Oberlin Conservatory in Ohio. Here, as one of only a few black students in the voice studios and dormitories in the mid-1980s, this gifted mezzo-soprano often felt alone, just as she did in the equally rarefied environments of the New England Conservatory of Music and the Houston Grand Opera. Through those trying times and ever since, she has felt a quiet humility as she receives ovations from the stages of opera houses worldwide.

Ten months out of the year, Denyce and David are on a grueling schedule of travel, rehearsals, and performances, living and working out of hotel rooms and opera houses in Vienna, Paris, San Francisco, Berlin, London, Florence, Zurich, Los Angeles, Houston, and New York, where Denyce opened the Metropolitan Opera's 1997 season in a widely acclaimed performance of *Carmen*. Their Leesburg home, which they bought in 1994, is their retreat. The open land that surrounds the house, as well as its convenience to Dulles Airport, are important, Denyce says. But mostly she enjoys a private tranquility here that had heretofore remained beyond her reach.

The 5,500-square-foot residence, the work of Loudoun County, Virginia, builder James Athey, is typical of the best and largest suburban tract houses built during the last twenty years. The exterior architectural design is a contemporary neocolonial rendition of the high style popular in the early twentieth century. The interior opens into fantastical and vivid rooms created by Denyce and David.

The first time the opera star walked into the two-story house, she experienced an immediate aversion to all the right angles typical features of neocolonial central-hall plans and especially of modern-day home-building. She also realized that this was to be her home for many years and proceeded to ask her husband, "Can't you do something to soften the squares?" Together they did, and to great effect.

The entrance opens into a large foyer, flowing into the living room and dining room and sweeping up the grand staircase, seemingly a three-dimensional stage set of classically inspired scenes. Full-size iron gates, which Denyce scavenged from an Atlanta flea market, screen the dining room threshold. Walls painted to depict Venetian scenes of doves and drapes, pastures and mountain valleys, mask the stairway wall leading to the second-floor bedrooms. The landing is anchored by a bronze sculpture of conductor Julius Rudell, an influential person in Denyce's life.

Lacquered lavender paint covers the walls in the downstairs den and piano room, where Denyce and David spend most of their time when they are home. The den looks out to the swimming pool and David's office, a detached, book-lined room containing two cherished Italian drawings, a gift from producer Franco Zefferelli, one of his 1963 stage setting for *La Boheme*, and another of *Three Sisters* from 1952. The piano room is shrouded in the light of a leaded-glass wall from Milan, veiling the kitchen on the other side.

The entrance foyer opens into the dining room (opposite) and living room (below) and up the grand staircase. Full-size iron gates, which Denyce scavenged from an Atlanta flea market, screen the dining room threshold. Walls are painted with Venetian scenes of doves, drapes, pastures, mountain valleys.

THEO ADAMSTEIN & OLVIA DEMETRIOU HOUSE

1940s | Builder Unknown
Renovated 1990 | A & D Design

Architects and interior designers Theo Adamstein and Olvia Demetriou completely demolished, redesigned, and rebuilt the interior of a generic 1940s neocolonial house, opening up interiors and saving only the central hearth in the dining room.

WITH ITS RUSTICATED STUCCO SURFACE COLORED IN THE WARM GOLD TONES OF ITALIAN STONE, THE FOXHALL RESIDENCE OF DESIGNERS THEO ADAMSTEIN AND OLVIA DEMETRIOU MIGHT WELL HAVE BEEN TRANSPLANTED FROM A TUSCAN HILL VILLAGE. YET THE HOUSE HAS STOOD IN THIS SUBURBAN NEIGHBORHOOD OF THE DISTRICT FOR DECADES, ORIGINALLY A GENERIC, GABLE-ROOFED HOUSE (FONDLY DERIDED BY LOCALS AS PSEUDO-COLONIAL) THAT REPRESENTED THE EPITOME OF THE AMERICAN DREAM AFTER THE 1920S. WITH THE RISE OF THE AUTOMOBILE, AS WELL AS WASHINGTON'S WORLD WAR II EMPLOYMENT BOOM, SPECULATIVE BUILDERS OBLIGINGLY FED THE VORACIOUS DEMAND FOR

The living room reflects the owners' design aesthetic, blending simple forms, warm tones, and historical references with contemporary open spaces, geometric shapes, and processional vistas.

these modest brick-and-frame uprights to ribbon the city's middle-class neighborhoods in outlying northwest and northeast districts. A half-century later, many of these houses remain virtually unchanged, except perhaps for postmodern additions of kitchens and family rooms.

Another exception is the house that Theo Adamstein and Olvia Demetriou bought in 1989 for its redevelopment potential and for the craggy, overgrown yard. The sole appeal of the house itself was its domestic scale and gabled roof, traditional features that express a sense of hearth and home to these owners. This strong domestic strain appears to grow out of their own histories. The couple's life together began in the

late 1970s when they were architecture students at the Cooper Union in New York. Each had arrived in the United States from a different culture and continent. Theo came from Cape Town, South Africa, in 1978, to finish his architecture schooling, bringing with him indigenous customs of a modernized colonial past. Olvia's father brought his family to America from Athens in 1963, when he ran the stateside office of a Greek architecture firm. Their fifteen-year marriage has proven to be a lucrative partnership, having produced a highly successful film-processing business in Georgetown as well as their equally successful architecture and interior design firm, A & D Design.

A & D's unique aesthetic blends the cozy (simple forms, warm tones, and historical references) and the contemporary (open spaces, geometric

Adamstein and Demetriou's style is replete with references to Theo's Southern African and Olvia's Mediterranean roots. Front to back, from the open kitchen (above) where they love to cook with friends, to the living room, "where we felt we could open up," says Theo, every room in the house is visually connected.

The view from the dining room up the stairwell to the second-floor bedrooms is a succession of processional scenes moving through the architecture, evoking a sense of discovery. Theo and Olvia's designs are reductionist, rather than formal and decorous, emphasizing the flow of space and the interplay between positive, negative, and geometrical spaces.

shapes, and processional vistas). Theo and Olvia think of their work as reductionist rather than formal or decorous. Their own house emphasizes the flow of space between rooms and the interplay between positive, negative, and geometrical spaces (the triangular gable, rectangular rooms, the trapezoid-shaped pool). Deep, calming tones abound, derived from the Mediterranean landscape. Soft grays, greens, and blues inside are complemented by the golden stucco exterior. Their signature style, whether working for a commercial or residential client, is replete with references to their European and South African roots. It is the simplicity of their architecture that welcomes this personal expression, as evidenced in several of their award-winning interiors for such trendy restaurants as Raku, Club Z, Coco Loco, and Provence.

Most of A & D Design's work, however, involves renovations, including their own former Georgetown town house. Here in Foxhall they had no qualms about gutting the original cookie-cutter colonial. They tore down the original walls to open up circulation within and out to the garden, and installed transparent garagelike doors in the living room that open onto the pool terrace, which spans the entire rear. The basic exterior form remained, turning the gable end from side to front facing the street, with a two-story addition for the living room and second-floor master bedroom suite at the back.

Here is the Adamstein-Demetriou household's most private space, inside and out, and it is playful. "The back is where we felt we could open up," explains Theo. Their master suite, a white-light treehouse of a bedroom and cobalt blue ceramic bath, emphasizes the sensuality of simple forms and of materials—white walls and ceiling, gable skylights above, private (yet not-so-private) slatted pocket doors reminiscent of African tribal masks, and translucent sand-blasted windows all around. It was Theo's photographer's eye that envisioned, then created, successive processional scenes as one moves through the architecture, evoking a sense of discovery.

Front to back, from the open kitchen where they love to cook with friends and the living room where they entertain, to the patio and pool where the children play, everyone is visually and experientially connected. This openness and certitude about where one is and where one is going is just what they intended. "The home is a place that has a real stability," Olvia says. "It provides a unique sense of permanence, timelessness, tapping into the ideal imagery of what home is."

CARL & NANCY GEWIRZ HOUSE

1979–89 | *Cesar Pelli*

*Architect Cesar Pelli
designed his first residence
for Carl and Nancy
Gewirz. The leaded copper
gable (above) forms the
horizontal roofline of Pelli's
"long gallery," the lineal
spine from which all
room pavilions flow. The
long gallery is the
dominant space of non-
specific function, says
Pelli, collecting and
directing movement like a
public street.*

DURING THEIR FORTY-YEAR MARRIAGE, CARL AND NANCY GEWIRZ HAVE BUILT THREE HOUSES IN WASHINGTON, D.C. THE MOST RECENT, DESIGNED BY CESAR PELLI, IS AS IMPORTANT TO THE DEVELOPMENT OF AMERICAN HOUSE DESIGN AS IT IS TO THE GEWIRZES' DAILY COMFORT. THROUGHOUT, THE SPACES ARE CHEERFUL AND LIGHT, MODERN YET TRADITIONAL, A GENUINE PLEASURE TO THE SENSES. AND THE HOUSE EMBODIES A REVEALING STORY ABOUT THE COLLABORATION BETWEEN THE PATRON AND THE ARCHITECT.

IN THE LAST DECADE CESAR PELLI HAS BECOME RECOGNIZED AS ONE OF THE LEADING INTERNATIONAL ARCHITECTS OF THE TWENTIETH CENTURY. HIS MOST NOTABLE MAJOR BUILDINGS INCLUDE THE WORLD TRADE CENTER IN NEW YORK

(1980–88), the Pacific Design Center in West Hollywood, California (1984), and the new National Airport in Washington, D.C. (1997). Known as a practical designer, he creates buildings that suit the needs of each client through the arrangement of spaces, circulation, room shapes, materials, colors, and technical systems. Born and educated in Argentina, Pelli arrived in the United States in 1950 to study at the University of Illinois' school of architecture. Later, he worked as an associate to Eero Saarinen for a decade, then as a partner with Gruen Associates in Los Angeles. In 1976, he established Cesar Pelli & Associates in New Haven with two partners and also began teaching at Yale University. Aside from a less formal pedagogical role with clients and associates, Pelli's most direct role as a mentor has been in the classroom, at Argentina's University of Tucuman, the University of California at Los Angeles, and as the dean of Yale's architecture school from 1977 to 1984.

For all the remarkable projects Pelli had designed, by the time he began working with the Gewirzes in 1979, he had yet to design a house. Carl and Nancy Gewirz, two people fiercely dedicated to all their creative endeavors who had interviewed and rejected a handful of stellar designers before coming to Pelli, were drawn to the artistry of his buildings and his accommodating nature.

"A lot of modern houses are extremely cold," says Nancy Gewirz, an antique textiles dealer, sculptor, and painter. "I wanted a beautiful house." The two-level house, like the garden room, is wonderfully bright with glass-walled geometries and light oak trim.

"A lot of modern houses are extremely cold," Nancy Gewirz explains. "I wanted a beautiful house." She and Carl also wanted a house that did not look like a particular style. The architecture grew out of both Pelli's and the Gewirzes' visions. Yet there was a detour along the way. Nancy and Carl had previously bought another site in Glen Echo, Maryland, that overlooked the Potomac River, for which Pelli had already designed one residence (stylistically rather different from their current residence). Three years into design, with construction drawings ready to go out for bid, Nancy stood out on the site one day and realized that the airplane overflights, as they made their final approaches into National Airport, were unbearable. They needed a quieter place to live. Within weeks, they found the site in Bethesda, and Pelli set out in a whole new direction.

The design concept of the Gewirzes' current house stemmed from Pelli's thinking back to ideas he had had about the nature of architecture in the early 1960s: places are designed for specific and nonspecific uses. At the time he was planning Comsat's corporate campus in suburban Maryland and sought to create a central area, a spine, "a place where people congregate like Main Street," he says today, "a place of intense social activity." About a decade later, in 1976, Pelli was asked to design a hypothetical house for an exhibition at the Venice Biennale. He organized a series of functions along a central lineal space, a street, which became the dominant space within a theoretical composi-

The living-room pavilion exemplifies the beauty of simple architectural shapes in natural materials. The Gewirzes' authentic English arts-and-crafts furniture, tapestries and objects furnish the simple geometry of the architecture.

tion. He refined the concept further in the Long Gallery House, a design for a 1980 exhibition by several contemporary architects at the Leo Castelli Gallery in New York, "Houses for Sale."

Cesar Pelli's long gallery came to fruition in the Gewirz house. (Cesar Pelli & Associates have since designed a second residence based on the long gallery principle in Jackson Hole, Wyoming.) The long gallery appeals to people because it is a natural solution to instinctual human patterns of use and activity. "We divide human functions in many ways: places where people do specific things, other places where people do many different things," he explains. "Porches in Mediterranean countries have done this for thousands of years." Transplanted to England, the gallery moved indoors, from which Pelli adapted his long gallery form, making it generously large for any function. It collects and directs movement like a public street, with the pavilions (private rooms) on either side. The satellite pavilions house specific uses and define the building type by their functions: a house, a campus, perhaps a museum or a school. The Gewirz house is a house, Nancy Gewirz says, "because the modules we picked are house modules: living room, dining room, kitchen, bedrooms, bathrooms, garage." They use the gallery as a "Main Street" of

Darker materials in the gallery (red brick, natural oak, and blue-gray British slate at the entrance) suggest the permanence of the spine, set against the lighter materials and smaller forms of the pavilions, which house flexible functions and changing uses. Sun streams in through the clerestory windows at the gallery's roof eave (Carl's idea), creating a marvelous view from the mezzanine of the second-floor master bedroom suite at one end looking out to the gallery's geometric truss framing, and sparkling pool and garden beyond.

sorts as the architect intended, mostly crossing from one side to the other, from the kitchen and dining room pavilions to the stairway and elevator leading to their second-floor suite of rooms. Large parties in the long gallery can become quite dramatic in the creative Gewirz household.

Throughout the design process, Pelli engaged the Gewirzes, drawing on their individual talents—Nancy an antique textiles dealer, sculptor, and painter, Carl a savvy real estate developer with a fine aesthetic eye. They spent a great deal of time during design in his New Haven office, where Pelli's associates systematically profiled the Gewirzes' personalities to get the house design and interior flow just right. The discovery continued down to the very last stage. During final design, the Gewirzes were traveling in Italy and noticed how important the "connectors" of La Rotunda in Vicenza were to the flow between the primary and secondary spaces. They called Pelli from Venice and convinced him to enlarge and deepen the connectors in their house to emphasize the transition spatially from the gallery into each pavilion.

Each room is an artistic creation of architecture, art, and the Gewirzes' fine English arts and crafts furniture. Among the most personal rooms, for the architect and the Gewirzes, is the dining room, a folly of a space that Pelli originally designed exclusively for formal occasions. Yet this wonderfully bright, glass-walled hexagon is intimate enough for two people (now they eat all their meals here) and large enough for ten. Pelli designed the ceiling's moderne art deco stencil, a take-off on the 1920s cherubic candelabra, a Parisian classic hanging from the center dome, "Cesar's modern interpretation of a million little cherubs," Nancy says fondly.

The long gallery's traditional gable roof of leaded copper is the dominant feature of the house. Darker materials in the 132-foot long gallery (red brick and natural oak) and the blue-gray British slate entrance with teak pergola suggest strength, stability, and the permanence of the spine set against the impermanence of the pavilions made of white stucco, clear glass, and lighter oak trim. In many respects, this residence is quite simple in form and feature: Architectural shapes in natural materials play against light and processional vistas. Sun streams in through clerestory windows at the gallery's roof eave (Carl's idea) seeming to permeate the entire house and creating a marvelous view from the mezzanine of the second-floor master bedroom suite at one end, through the gallery's geometric truss framing, and out to a sparkling pool and garden. The Gewirzes requested the second level for their bedroom–sitting room suite, which required Pelli to readapt the long gallery's pure one-level composition to the realities of the building's function and, of course, the Gewirzes themselves. Rising to two stories, in fact, created marvelous vistas. "You are always looking back on the architecture," says Carl, through the procession

GERMAN AMBASSADOR'S RESIDENCE

1994 | *Oswald Mathias Ungers*

The monumental columned portico expresses the dignified rationalistic design of the American residence of the German Ambassador, Juergen Chrobog and his wife, Magda Gohar-Chrobog. Architect Oswald Mathias Ungers created an impressive (and controversial) modern building that combines Renaissance principles of representational space, scale, and ornament with colossal forms of polished white stone, ebony trim, and bleached oak.

THE GERMAN AMBASSADOR'S RESIDENCE, A MONUMENTAL, RATIONALISTIC VILLA SET ON A HILL, TELLS AS MUCH ABOUT THE IMPORTANCE OF GERMANY'S TIES TO AMERICA AS IT DOES ABOUT GERMAN ART AND ARCHITECTURE IN THE 1990S. AFTER TWELVE YEARS OF PLANNING AND TWO DESIGN COMPETITIONS, THIS DIPLOMATIC RESIDENCE INDEED EXPRESSES "THE GREAT IMPORTANCE WHICH THE FEDERAL REPUBLIC OF GERMANY ASCRIBES TO ITS RELATIONS WITH THE UNITED STATES," AS KLAUS KINKEL, MINISTER OF FOREIGN AFFAIRS, SAID IN 1995.

ARCHITECT OSWALD MATHIAS UNGERS HAD SEEN MUCH OF THE AMERICAN LANDSCAPE DURING HIS LONG TENURES AS PROFESSOR AND CHAIR

of the architecture department at Cornell, and as professor at Harvard and UCLA. Since opening his first architecture office in Cologne in 1950 (another followed in Berlin in 1964), he has become one of Germany's most eminent architects. His formalist skyscrapers and government buildings are characterized by dynamic shifts in scale and proportion. But even as he designs in the modernist tradition, he embraces the classical precepts of the sixteenth century.

For the ambassador's residence the architect envisioned a Roman villa grounded in Renaissance principles of representational space, scale, and ornament. Through the columned entrance portico, the great reception hall draws guests into the ceremonial center, a double-height space under a vaulted ceiling. Contained space bursts open in a brilliant mix of sunlight from the south portico's glass wall and overhead fluorescent panels that illuminate white walls and the polished white stone and bleached hardwood floors. At the end of the hall, oversize glass doors open out to the portico, terrace, and garden below. Every architectural detail reinforces the residence's colossal scale: door handles are positioned high and seem more compatible with those of a massive castle than a private domicile.

Early in the design, the architect chose artist Markus Lupertz to create a frieze of woodcuts on canvas: twelve faces of Parsifal to keep watch over the great hall. From the beginning, Ungers intended that this great white house function as a canvas for artists and the landscape designer. Introducing other artistic personalities into the rigid architectural scheme required great care, by Ungers and the artists, and the integration makes the vast building appear more humane and welcoming. It is a *Gesamtkunstwerk*, Ungers explains, a unified work of art and architecture.

The landscape design is the crowning glory that fulfills the promise of the

Ungers intended the great white house's function to be a Gesamtkunstwerk, *a unified work of art and architecture, introducing murals by Gerhard Merz (opposite) and paintings by Christa Naher, Rosemarie Trockel, Simon Ungers, and Markus Lupertz into his scheme.*

Landscape architect Bernhard Korte preserved the natural topography, with the portico on the hilltop of the south terrace, leading down two parallel flights of stairs to the park and lower terrace of a reflecting pool and vine trellis.

*In the family's private
quarters modern materials
(handcrafted steel hinges
and polished marble and
granite floors) are juxtaposed
with fine European antique
furniture and tapestries.*

architectural design. Landscape architect Bernhard Korte preserved the natural topography of the old Averell Harriman estate. From the hilltop on the south terrace, two parallel flights of stairs lead down to the park and follow the slope of the hill to a lower terrace with a reflecting pool and vine trellis. The symmetry of the park and parallel stairways rises from the serene garden at the lowest point to the monumental columned portico at the highest, then releases and unfolds around the residence through a landscape of winding paths.

In a rare stricture for embassies in America, the ambassador and his family are contractually obliged to consult Ungers if they wish to move furniture and art in the ceremonial rooms—any painting on any wall, any chair in any room, even a petite Hochst china figurine or silver utensil. Ungers saw every detail in the context of a precise system of geometry that dictated the design of window panes, the inlaid granite, the marble and parquet floors, cube chairs, handcrafted steel hinges, doorknobs, and door keys. Even Korte's plantings respect the geometric regime, with cone-shaped evergreen magnolias and hedges outlining the terraces and the square, trellised pavilion anchoring the lower garden. Following the house's rationalistic composition, gardeners crop the wild wisteria so that it hugs the cubic trellises.

Yet since the house opened in 1994 it has been brutally criticized in the architect's home country: a *Teutonenklotz,* a teutonic block, said one source; cold, brutal, a complete lack of domestic atmosphere, said another. The American press has been far less severe. When Ambassador Juergen Chrobog and Magda Gohar-Chrobog arrived in Washington the following year, they came with mixed emotions. They were thrilled to return to an embassy post after a twelve-year hiatus yet, from all reports, expected the worst in their new home. "We were positively surprised," Ambassador Chrobog admits. Their response endeared them to Ungers, who began to relax his rigid standards and even permitted the Chrobogs certain freedoms in interpreting the original interior design in official rooms. "He let us do things" to add warmth to the rooms, says Gohar-Chrobog, such as arranging chairs to face one another to encourage conversation. The ambassador and his wife have added a silk oriental rug in the great hall, porcelain figurines on the grand piano and in the salon, and a cool Impressionist painting in the ladies' sitting room. They even joined the architect and the expressionist painter Bernard Schultze to select four large works for the dining room and one major piece for the entrance hall. In the private living quarters on the second floor, a commodious four thousand square feet, the Chrobogs and their three sons have filled the white, gallery-like space with exquisite European antiques.

The ambassador's residence may be controversial, but as a symbol of German architectural and artistic achievement, it responds with certain boldness to its many purposes as national calling card, ceremonial hall, and home.

INDEX